The CHANGE Perspective

Insights in Change and Development

Dedicated to my wife,
Terry de Zoete

Martijn de Zoete

Colofon

Author: Martijn de Zoete
The CHANGE Perspective
Insights in Change and Development

First print: September 2017

ISBN: 9789460510885
NUR: 801

Design by Logo Shop, www.logo-shop.nl
Correction by Terry de Zoete
A publication of Attrakt BV, www.attrakt.nl

Index

This is Roy van Bergen. Director-owner of RTech, a high-tech production company. RTech develops and produces parts, that are used in the production process of other companies. Sometimes RTech customizes these parts as they have to meet very specific requirements. For some customers they produce large quantities of "disposables" for the production lines. As a result of the loss of a very big customer RTech is undergoing a change process, which has a huge impact on both the internal as well as the external environment of the organisation. Join Roy during this radical development process. At the same time, we will explain all the things that are happening using the Z-model of change®.

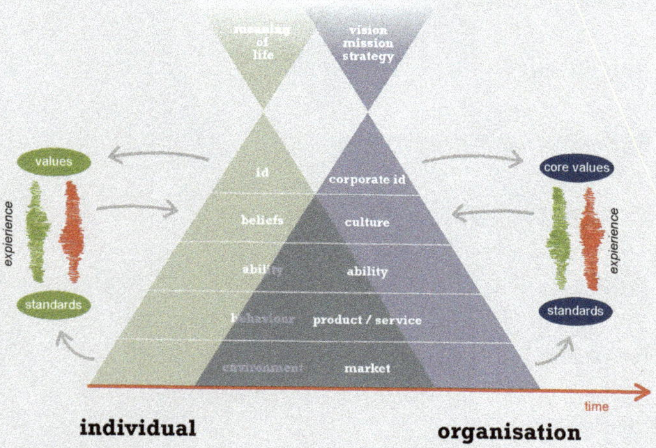

The development model is based on Dilts and Bateson's logical levels, which shows the position of an individual within the environment, behaviour, ability, beliefs, identity and fulfilment levels. De Zoete integrates this concept into the corporate world, thus showing an organisation within the market (environment), product/service (behaviour), ability, culture (beliefs), company identity and vision-mission-strategy (fulfilment) levels. The overlap between the individual and the organisation is of the utmost importance, as are the values, standards and experiences that both the individual (green) as well as the organisation (blue) gain and, if necessary, respond to. Three short video-clips give you the opportunity to become familiar with the Z-model of change® and you will be able to see the effects of the shifts that emerge during the process of change.

Movie 1

Movie 2

Movie 3

1 Reality check

Change is present, always and everywhere. Although we do not always realise how incredibly flexible we actually are, we easily adapt to things like the Internet, mobile phones etcetera. However, we sometimes have issues coping with bigger changes.

Changes constantly occur all around us in our everyday lives. Climate change, political change like Brexit, technological change, artificial intelligence, changes in energy. These are exciting and for some frightening times. We love being flexible, without being forced to change.
The concept of change is difficult for most people. Yet, when you have the insight in how change actually works, you can consider change to be a natural phenomenon. This will allow you to explain and reflect on change as such. Then you will be able to take responsibility for the results of changes that were initiated in the past and take effect now.

To make the philosophical concept of change understandable for most people, I chose to write a business novel as a metaphor for this concept. Since change is present always and everywhere, it can be translated from an individual change into a team development program and subsequently into organisational change.

Yesterday the world was at your feet, today you have entered into a violent storm. You have gone from endless profits to unsolvable deficits in no time. From quietly keeping on track to mobilising all your efforts. That does not make any sense. Of course, it does not. Yet this is what reality looks like to many organisations. RTech is by no means an exception. The company

hit it off right from the beginning. The company started out as a hobby of a college student ran from an attic room. Within 5 years, it had grown from a one-man business into a professional, high-tech company with four hundred employees. A solid, multidisciplinary organisation, with a low turnover of both customers and staff. Too small to run for the 'best employer of the year' award, but employee satisfaction was far beyond average. Customer satisfaction was even better. Renowned companies have committed themselves to RTech and they are rightly proud of that. RTech's knowledge and experience seem hard to match, the competition remains far behind. All the evidence suggests that this is truly a formula for success.
Still, something is keeping Roy, the owner of the company, up night after night some ten years later. He is forced to make a radical and irreversible decision. He is feeling stressed out and confused while searching for a solution to survive this crisis. To save his company and limit the damage. On the eve of what appears to be an impossible choice, he can only see one way out: bankruptcy.

2 Company on fire

4 a.m., an endless monologue. Continuous and relentlessly disturbing. Fifteen years. It does not make sense. It cannot be. All my efforts, all for nothing? Fifteen years. I built a company from scratch: RTech. My company: Roy Technology. A company that transformed a wealth of technology into high performance technological products. Dreams turned into reality. A leader in its segment. Successful from the very first handshake. Time and time again, clients placed large orders and signed contracts. I did not go to the client, the client came to me. 400 employees. 400! And now? Into the red. Nothing but losses. For months now they have been screaming to get my attention, but I did not want to know. I still do not. I have tried everything within my power to turn the tide, but I mostly succeeded in ignoring them. It'll be fine, I kept on saying. But I am afraid it won't be fine. Something has to change. Something will change. I have to do something about this crisis, but what? What?

What happened? How could this have happened? How could this have happened to me? My company? My success? It was all going so well. In fact, ridiculously well. Last year for example, I took all my business relations to the World Cup in Brazil. Anything was possible! Should I have sounded the alarm sooner? Intervened sooner? Now everything is lost. Everything is ruined. There is nothing left. Why? Why me? This shouldn't have happened. I was so successful. Why did not I see what was coming? Why did I not…

I leave for the office far too early, my heart was in my mouth. I stare at an imaginary spot on my desk, without reading a word of the numerous documents that keep piling up. Suddenly I find myself going through my digital address book, looking for a long forgotten phone number. When I hang up, I realise that I have done all the talking. But within an hour my secretary calls and lets me know my appointment has arrived: Max.

More than 10 years have gone by since I have last spoken to him. The one person that was always there for me, for as long as I can remember. Who never quizzed me, never told me off, never belittled me. Who treated me as his equal, not like a toddler. The only one who put up with my adolescent behaviour. Who picked me up every time I fell down, without ever judging me. Who never once told me how stupid I had been... again. And the more I realised it myself... later on. I realise that I am curious to find out what type of expensive car he is driving now.. He always loved the fast cars and in this respect , as in many other things, he was very special. Ten years...

I am embarrassed, but I do not know what else to do. Nobody else to approach. Nobody else I can really trust. Nobody else to I can talk to about this. I do not want to cause panic within my company and talking about it at home is not an option either. Linda already has enough on her mind. After all, we do have a family to support. And I certainly do not want to talk about it with my friends. Never. They see me as this successful businessman and I would really like to keep it that way.

I quickly get rid of the lump in my throat. I get up and shake Max's hand. As usual, he greets me calmly and warmly. But still I do not know where to start. Should I get right down to business and talk about my debts? Or take a step back and fill up those fifteen years of radio silence? When Alice brings us our coffee, we still have not said a word to each other. Yet the silence that fills my office feels comfortable rather than painful. Max does not even look at me with an interrogative eye, but quietly walks around admiring my stylish office. The walls are white, as is the large bookshelf in the corner of the room. It is filled with books on technology and management and some miniature prototypes of our top range products. I could go on about those products for hours. For example, about the nozzles for industrial whipped cream dispensers that stay cleaner as a result of their shape. Therefore, the equipment needs to be cleaned less often. About the very beginning: how the idea emerged. About gathering the required knowledge and materials. Refining the technique. Fine-tuning the products. About the presentation of my first prototype. The investors' enthusiasm. The over the top sales figures. My own enthusiasm is getting a hold of me again, but just as I am about to tell him all about it, I shut my mouth again. It would only be postponing the inevitable.

> *To listen means more than just to wait for the other one to stop talking*
> ***J. van Dam***

Max is now standing right in the middle of my office, next to the large, solid oak wood conference table. My desk, which is also made from this beautiful type of wood, has a few piles of paper and a picture frame on it that holds a picture of my wife, my daughters and Puck, our Labrador retriever. It remains silent for quite some time. But at some point, I cannot take it any longer and start ranting, so that I don't explode. There is absolutely no question of saying things in chronological order, because I take huge leaps from the future to the past and back. It is a miracle Max does not make a run for it. Only afterwards, I realise that I have asked him loads of questions, non-stop. Both hopeful and desperate. But still I cannot remember any answers, let alone any kind of response to my story. He just let me rage and roar. Knowing Max, he hasn't just listened to every single word I said, but he has also taken each one of them very seriously. But I cannot remember any kind of response I have told him so many things. Mostly about my company; about the customers that paid top dollar but also about the mounting debts. About the chaos I am too afraid to face but no longer can ignore. I have even told him all the personal stuff. The successful man I used to be. But I have failed. What is left of me is small and insignificant. Broken. I am putting all my cards out on the table.

That beautiful dark table Max patiently rests his hands on, while mine are waving around restlessly. Only my elbows touch the heavy conference table when I bend forward and put my head to rest in my hands. Although the word 'rest' does not exactly apply to me. I do not sleep, I cannot concentrate. I can only focus on The Big Decision, but I cannot get to grips with it. Won't get to grips with it. Have to...
Silence remains. Again, no response. No redeeming words. No comprehensive solution.

I cannot stand this silence any longer. I get up and start an endless monologue yet again. I had seen it coming for months. Stupid, stupid, stupid that I did not act any sooner. I could have prevented so many things. Could have done so much more. Couldn't I? That one big customer should have changed his point of view. Should have stayed with us. Then none of this would have happened. I still do not understand. Why did my biggest customer switch to the competition? We got a 6.3 at our latest customer satisfaction research and that is enough, isn't it? RTech delivers better quality, so the price difference really is acceptable. It always has been. Not to mention our service and reliability. And you should be able to expect some brand loyalty of your customers and...

Max lets me go on and on about all my stupidities with the same patience as he did an hour and a half ago. Listens to all the things I chose to ignore. And how that is no longer an option now. I think that was the moment Max finally spoke for the first time.

> *'Choosing not to make a decision is also a decision, Roy. Only then the decision is made for you.'*

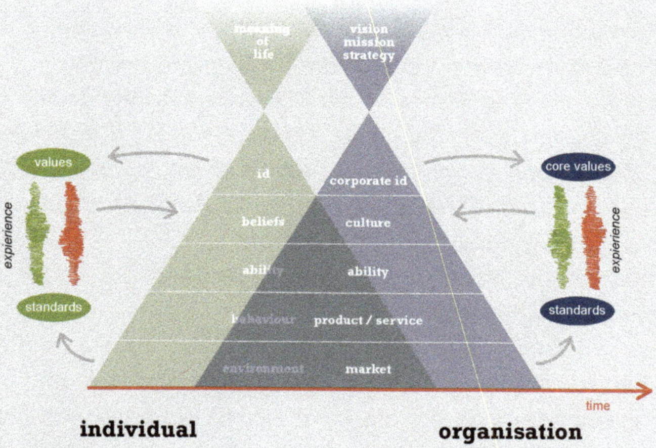

What is happening?

In an organisation the work is done by employees. In fact, an organisation is nothing more than a collection of people working together towards a common goal. In the model the individual is represented by the green part of the model. The organisation is represented by the blue part.

When we look at the model in a stable situation, we see that the individual (green) and the organisation (blue) partially overlap. What is remarkable however, is that the identity (ID) of an individual does not have any overlap with the identity of the organisation he or she works for. Both identities are unique and in no way equal to each other, although this is often assumed and experienced. In other words: a person is always more than an individual in his or her organisation and an organisation is always more than just one person. The same goes for the self-employed. Just think about the non-work-related spare time of the entrepreneur. And all the possible tasks he or she performs reluctantly or maybe even outsources.

Theoretically we are aware of this. However, in actual practice things often appear quite differently. Such blending can have big consequences for both the professional as well as the personal performance.

The overlap between green (the individual) and blue (the organisation) in the model is called the role someone plays within an organisation. The overlap will get bigger, whenever someone is holding a more ideal position within an organisation. Each individual is always more than the assumed role he or she plays in a company. Just like an organisation is always more than the role that this person plays in it. The amount of overlap between green and blue depends on how well someone's role suits both the individual and the organisation. Should the role someone is playing suit the person but not the company, it will cause friction. Likewise, when the role someone plays does not suit the person him or herself. Whenever someone is holding a more ideal position within an organisation, the overlap will be bigger.

Reflection

Did you ever consider if you are in the right place with the role you currently fulfil? It is easy to gain some insight in that topic, by answering the following questions. The most challenging part is just to be honest.

Answer the following questions with the values 1,2,3,4, and 5. 1 represents "total disagreement", 3 represents "neutral" and 5 represents "total agreement".

1 I regularly do things because I am asked to do so, without knowing why it is important.
2 I do have issues doing certain parts of my job, because I do not have the competences and knowledvge to do those parts really well.
3 To be honest, I do not always like the ethos in my job
4 Things that really matter to me in my personal life are not reflected in my job.
5 I often get the feedback that "it has to be done better"

When you score 12 points or less, you really are a good fit for your role. Between 12 and 18 points indicates that there is room for improvement. 18 points or higher means you might ask yourself the question "is this job right for me?"

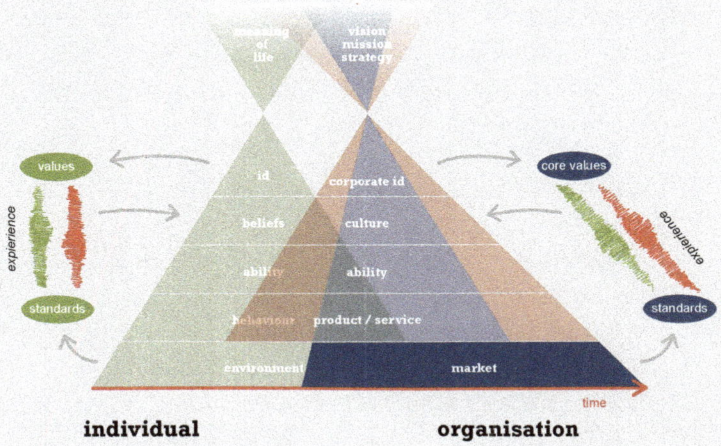

What is happening?

The organisation of Roy Technology is, just like any other company, in an environment which is continuously changing. A customer left RTech because RTech couldn't fulfil their needs at some point. In the model, this change is shown by the shifted dark blue area, which marks the level of the market. As a consequence, the interface between this level and the next higher level becomes smaller, which is the level of products and services. So, the products and services provided by RTech no longer fully meet the needs of the market. This increases the risk of losing customers. And this is what is actually happening here. One of RTech's main customers has left, which subsequently leads to a drastic decrease in profits.

Reflection

Of course, it is useful to know if your market is in motion, so you can monitor your risks. Ask yourself the following question:

1 Which competitors show more growth than I do?

2 Which products and services from my portfolio are barely sold? What is the cause?
3 Which products and services show a significant decrease in turnover? What is the cause? Quantities or a lower price?
4 Which products and services are stable? What is the cause?
5 Are you sure about the reasons you gave in question 4 or are they merely based on your assumptions?
6 Which products and services could you add to your portfolio that might improve customer relationships or create cross/deep sell possibilities? Which competitors sell these products and services? And what is the reason that you do not?

If you can't answer three of the above questions within one day, you can safely assume that you have a higher risk on changes in your market that will not be beneficial for your revenue.

I did not take his response into account for one second. I can come up with a hundred things that keep me from making these decisions. Applying for bankruptcy is a big thing. So is the alternative, a huge wave of dismissals. There are numerous things that I really should do first, like analysing our sales data which we have never looked at. How do I make the right choices? There are dozens of reasons why I shouldn't make this decision at all. I just do not know the correct order! What comes first and what comes next? No, I cannot make choices now. Not now. Not me. But there is no other way, I do realise that. It is not easy, but I do have to make decisions. Impossible decisions I have put off far too long, hoping the solution would come naturally. But that is no longer an option. I take a deep breath and am fully aware that I am on the eve of making a decision that will inevitably cause memorable changes. Not just for me, but for all my employees. And for each and every one around them. It takes a while for me to exhale. Are we going down completely or will we bravely make it through the dark days? Is reanimation still an option or is all hope lost? When my eldest daughter goes to high school in a few years, will her dad still be half the man he used to be? Are we just heading for a few months of revalidation or do I really have to look for another career? These numerous unanswered questions make my head spin, but I am too scared to learn the answers. With the deep inhalation still floating high up in my chest, I am standing still, too scared to move. Max has to help me. His knowledge and years of experience must result in solutions. To everything. I look at Max in complete confidence. But again, it remains silent.

I am scared to break this silence. My faith in Max remains. Hours seem to pass. For minutes, it remains silent. Until Max firmly says:

> *'I am not here to bring you the answers Roy.*
> *I am here to ask you difficult questions.*
> *You will come up with the answers yourself.*
> *Have faith that you will.'*

Have faith? In what? I look at Max with a questioning face, realising that indeed I expect him to come up with the answers. That I expect not to be able to make it without his solutions. The decisions, the consequences. Everything. My company, my employees, what lies ahead of us? How can I go on when I do not know how to? If Max does not show me how. There is no silence now whatsoever. I go out of my way to convince Max that there is an urgent issue waiting for him. That I have turned to him for a very good reason. I want to put my destiny in his hands, make use of his experience, want to be helped by him. So many people depend on him solving this. Him dealing with this. Max fixing this. I do not know whether it is the insomnia or my fear that this is really going to be the end of my company. And of my personal leadership. My persuasiveness leaves much to be desired. Max stays calm. Even when I have convinced myself that he cannot evade giving a response, he starts speaking cryptically and I have lost him again.

> *'Each question is like a unique puzzle. The only suitable answers are those that come from the same origin as the question itself. Even when it seems like all the pieces have gone missing.*
>
> *I cannot give you the pieces, Roy. But I can help you find them.'*

I looked at him in confusion. But despite my inimitable expectation, despite my hope for the subtitles of yet another quote I do not understand, Max takes out his agenda and we make a follow-up appointment.

> *'At this moment, what is our top priority? For example, if a building is going up in flames, that consideration is obvious: how much attention do you spend on finding the cause of the fire, before taking out the hose?*

While I am walking towards my desk to consult my digital agenda, it is Max who finally starts talking. We will refrain from

If an organisation wants to change with the market and wants to connect with customer needs, it has to move into the red surfaces of the model. The left side of the blue pyramid shows that the company has to get rid of old products and services, old machines and employees who do not fit their role anymore. They are unable to change their mindset and should be replaced by employees who are more competent, to ensure the future of the company.

On the right side of the model, representing the future, new things are demanded by the market. Call it improvement. Better yet. Call it innovation. New products, new machines, new employees.

What is literally happening in this metaphor is that the market has shifted. RTech loses a product (left red surface on the level of product) and does not have an alternative product (right red surface on the level of product). As a result, machines do not produce and employees are waiting to get fired. The common belief "RTech is top" does not appear to be true at this point in time.

If we look more closely at the consequences for the individual Roy, we find that the changed organisational environment leads to the need for new personal beliefs for Roy. Doing nothing is not an option, and his personal belief that he has insufficient knowledge to deal with this situation caused him to call Max.

Looking closer at Roy's personality, we see that he is fighting change. But as long as his beliefs are focussed on maintaining the old situation, he will not be able to be of service to the changing organisation. He and his ego will then be stuck in the great past and he won't be able to develop. Roy has to go along with the changing organisation. Put aside his ego and start playing his role. The directing role.

If you want to be a leader to others, become your own master first
P. Massinger

In order to survive as a company, it is necessary to accept the present and act on the short term (put out the fire). So, the company can develop (mop up) and start working on its future (build up). Rejecting Roy's individual interest (afraid to lose face in the short term) on behalf of the existence of the organisation is a crucial leadership quality that Max is stirring up in Roy.

Reflection

It is good to ask yourself about your ability to adapt to big changes that are forced upon you.

Ask yourself the following questions;

1 How would it affect me if my pay check was cut in half while my position and duties remained the same?
2 How would it feel if something really bad happens to my business? What would I do? Sit down and weep or get into action and think of this as the start of something new?
3 What would happen if my company grew twice as big in a year. Can I handle that? Can my organisation handle that?
4 How well prepared am I, concerning crisis situations? Do I know the facts? Do I know how to influence my organisation to move faster or to take a step back?
5 If I am being truly honest to myself: Does change happen to me or do I create change myself?

3 Put out the fire.

After the recent exit of one of my biggest customers, the revenue has almost halved. That alone is a disturbing development. But unfortunately, this did not automatically cause an equal decrease in personnel and production costs. On the contrary, they have remained at the same level as before the exit of this particular customer. As a consequence, the account deficits keep mounting and the reserves are declining. A situation with a short expiration date. High time to grab the fire hose and put out the fire.

Opening the water hose clearly means filling the financial gap. But that is easier said than done. We should cut the costs, but how? I cannot pull the plug out of the production line we ran specifically for the customer who abandoned us. It is too successful to throw in the towel. Too precious to be gathering dust on the shelf. 'So is there a demand for it then?' Max asks. 'Roy? Is there a demand for it?'. And then there is silence.

I call for an emergency meeting and discuss this with my sales team. We look at all the options for hours and hours. All the alternatives. And unfortunately, we all unanimously agree on one thing: there is no demand for this top product. Impossible and unbelievable. It is a high-quality product and no other company has the expertise that RTech has, to bring this unrivalled gem on the market. And yet I fear Max is right. If there is no demand for it, then we have to stop the production process. This way we won't be spending money on a product which, at this point, does not give a return. From a rational and logical point of view I support this decision all the way. And I do realise that we have to put out this fire, in order to save the rest of the company from burning down all together. But saying goodbye to the one product we once started off with, has major impact on me. It feels as if the floor is being swept away from underneath my feet. The true foundation of this company. The one product RTech owes all its' success to. Its' first success. The first stepping stone. The first overwhelming contracts. Its' first earned capital. Destroying this starting point feels like denying the success. Like having to fire your founder... is that truly the only solution?

Accept what is
Let go of what was
Have faith in what will be
(unknown)

So, we are saying goodbye to our first success. This means machines will be shut down, people will be out of a job. It means RTech will halve in size and will be more dependent on other customers. Customers who are still buying our other products. The consequences are still unknown. Though this is what we have to do. The costs are too high and each month we allow this situation to drag on, it will cost us enormous sums of money. There is no time to lose.

As the director, it is my job to act. Now. Irrevocably cut costs and say goodbye to half of my technical staff and sales managers. This is so much easier said than done. Just the thought of having to let go of my staff, people I have carefully selected and hired, makes me even more aware of the huge knot in my stomach.

I talk about this stressful experience with Max. He keeps his head cool. That makes it easier for him, he says, because it gives him the opportunity to look at the facts instead of the emotions that come along with stress. I ask him how he does that, because in my mind everything's a blur.

"Facts are things without emotions", Max says. "We suffer from the fact that we interpret the facts and this in turn evokes emotions. If we then act upon our emotions, we will make emotional decisions. However, making decisions merely based on facts and figures is not the alternative. Emotions have to be part of the mix. Emotions make us human. I only allow them to be added to the mix after I have developed a rational concept. By the way, that might be different for everybody. As long as you use your ratio and your emotion when making a decision, it is ok. Acting purely based on emotions is pretty risky, for example in your communication toward the unions, banks and other stakeholders. So, let us see how that works for you, so you can manage your stress level during your meetings with stakeholders. That will prevent you from making mistakes for RTech and yourself. Behaving calm and trustworthy in the communication with your employees is crucial at this point."

A second emergency meeting in as many weeks has led to a lot of distress within the company. The tension is palpable and when I announce a reorganisation, it comes as no surprise. The company had been a gathering place of job satisfaction, teamwork and contentment up until a few weeks ago. Now it was suddenly reduced to a place of anxiety, insecurity, mistrust and envy. Unfortunately, the remaining doubts I have as to the correctness of my decision, are not dispelled by anyone present. And I did not have any other choice. Still, the actual process of decision making has yet to start, for who is to stay and who is to abandon ship? For whom will the open arms of RTech close, just to sadly wave them goodbye? I cannot dissociate the question of who is to leave based on the changing production line from the support of my warm professional family. Who can do without me as an employer? Who can do without his job, income and existence? I am forced to say goodbye to some very good people. People who are going to pay big time for putting their trust in a top product. People who have made good decisions, which in the end turn out to be the worst they have ever made. It is not right. It is not fair. Not to them. And not to me, to be the instigator of several fires somewhere else, just so I can put out my own big fire. But there is no other way. I might be able to help them, get them started in another company. But still I will have to let go of a large part of their personal process.

The choices have been made and the names of the employees who will be dismissed are known. I get in my car to go and tell a few employees in person. The others will be informed as soon as I get back to the office. One by one they walk in, with hanging shoulders, only to leave my office even more nerve wrecked. Myself included at the end of this dreadful day. Never have I had to have such talks with my people, with anyone for that matter. Never have I been forced to fire this many people. Never thought it would be necessary. Never knew it would be this difficult. I would rather have let Max do these talks. He is probably better at it than I am. It is probably easier for him. I mean, he does not know them or anything. But they are not his people. I have to do this myself. They are part of my company, so they are part of me.

After informing everyone concerned, it is time for a short presentation to the entire company. I will tell them what is going on and what the consequences will be for them. But what will the consequences be for them? The anticipation of the numerous questions they will be firing at me, keeps me paralyzed with fear. Keeps me from entering the room where everyone is waiting for me. All of them feeling uneasy and impatient. Just as I am. I will not be able to answer many of their questions at this point. I vividly remember the feeling I had during the many talks I had with Max, in which he refused to answer my questions. But this is different. I actually do not have the answers. I am simply not capable of answering them, although I wished I had all the answers right up my sleeve. I would have loved to send all my employees off with their heads held high. Filled with hope and realistic expectations of a company that would overcome all its' issues and ensure them of their jobs and income. Ensured of renewed job satisfaction and confidence not only in each other but also in management. Enabling me to go home with my head held high tonight, confident that everything's going to be ok. That everything and everyone will be just fine.

Suddenly I realise that Max does not have all the answers either, but he does want to help me. My hopeful smile is fading into a fierce grimace. It feels as though everything is shaking and the danger of collapsing is still imminent. The door handle feels moist because of my clammy hand clinging on to it. On the other side of the door, the commotion is increasing. But when I open the door, it almost immediately turns into complete silence. Several hundred people look at me anxiously and restlessly. I intend to limit myself to the message I have written down, which I almost literally read aloud because of my nerves. I remain calm during the many, many questions I cannot answer and keep repeating the sentence Max and I came up with: 'I regret not being able to answer this question at the moment either, but I promise to keep you informed on all future developments. You can always step into my office.' There is no question of me keeping my head held high. Nor is there any question of hope, trust or any other positive emotion. Before I drive home, I take a small detour to Max. Just for a minute... I do not even know what I expect from him. No answers, no solutions. No satisfied employees or any other kind of hope.

But still Max is trying very hard to encourage me. 'We have put out the fire. We have taken decisions. Look at what you do have', Max keeps on repeating. 'It takes some effort, but it will be worth it in the end'. Despite everything, there is still a large part of my company left. Several production processes are still fully operation. They are serving the satisfied customer groups who are still buying the products. It is almost business as usual. Or something like that. The company's leftovers remain basically unchanged. My employees are doing their jobs as usual. The remaining buyers are still placing orders. This should mean that in the long run, a positive operating result should be developed. All's well that ends well? But still there is a lot to be done.

Mop up. 'First turn off the tap!', I can still hear Max saying that to me. I looked at him with glazy eyes when he said those bizarre words. As if I had woken up in one of those read-aloud books. It is only now that I understand what he was actually trying to say. Because all the mopping we have done the past period, has left us with a lot of waste. And as long as the tap is still open, we keep gathering waste. Reducing my staff by half had unfortunately just been step one.

Since having approached Max, I feel like I am in a roller coaster. Everything is happening too fast and at the same time I am oblivious to everything. It is making my head spin. I am leaving behind a beautiful landscape of products and potential clients. Going back is no option. Quitting is fatal. Carry on is the motto. Taking the express route to our final destination. But what is our destination? What are we headed towards? Is it really this foggy or am I just scared to polish my glasses? Is it such a rocky road or are my legs shaking with tension and inability? It does not take much more to lose myself in this endless stress spiral. However, reality is already knocking at my door again and I know I have to carry on. Max now mentions the company building. Is he serious? First my staff, now my building as well? With a great deal of sorrow, I admit that the building is too big for its' current utilisation. But I cannot let it go. Honestly, I cannot. It feels like only yesterday when I got the key to this beautiful building. I remember feeling so proud while walking through the endless hallways, making sure all offices were stylishly decorated, creating an inspiring working environment and welcoming employees and customers into my comfortable working space. A building that suits future expansion plans, which isn't so bad for a young adult who's still learning. Especially when taking into account the enormous growth spurt. Only now this huge building does not suit the grown man anymore.

It keeps on being a very painful journey. One that is taking too long, but at the same time takes too little time because everything keeps on happening at the same time. It seems as though all decisions need to be taken all at once. A hectic journey filled with painful moments of saying goodbye. It is not only hard for me having to say goodbye to the incomprehensive redundancy in human capital. It is also hard having to say farewell to every single brick I have used to build up my company. The technology I have designed to perfection bit by bit. The large conference table and the top book shelves, together with Peter. Peter is the man responsible for Production now, who joined RTech as the first employee 14 years ago, because he had so much technical knowledge I just had to hire him. He came up with so many great ideas, which also allowed RTech to grow. Without Peter things would have been different. Do I really have to say farewell to the big conference table and the ideas on the shelves? How I used to love everything that was on those shelves. Some plans and ideas were buried under a huge amount of dust, but still, they were there. Waiting for the right time. For the future. My future...

'Patience is the calm acceptance
that things can happen
in a different order than the one
you have in mind.'
David G. Allen

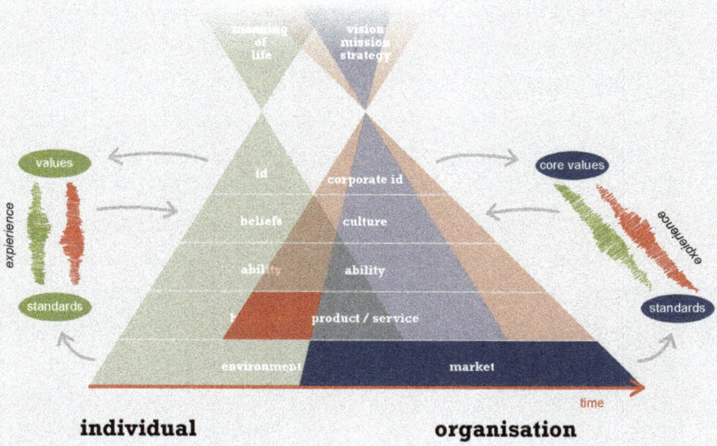

What is happening?

The market is changing. Customer needs are changing. By regularly talking to your customers you can anticipate what they are going to need. RTech is now paying for not sufficiently maintaining customer contact. Its' products and services no longer meet the needs of the largest customer, so they switched to the competition.

For the organisation this is crucial; will it find a market for its' products and services in the red area of the model, so the company remains to exist in its' current form? Or will it go with the flow of the changing market?

Looking at RTech, there is no longer a market for the 'red' products and services, so it will have to let these products go. This farewell is inevitable for the organisation, because it will enable the company to keep a keen eye on things.

Reflection

Answer the following questions to gain insight in your organisational risks

1 There are less than 10 clients Yes / No
2 One of my clients represents more than 30%

	of my turnover	Yes / No
3	If one of my two largest clients left, I would have a problem	Yes / No
4	I only have contact with my clients when they place an order	Yes / No
5	I do not talk about market developments with my clients	Yes / no

If you answered yes three times or more, you really are in a risky position.

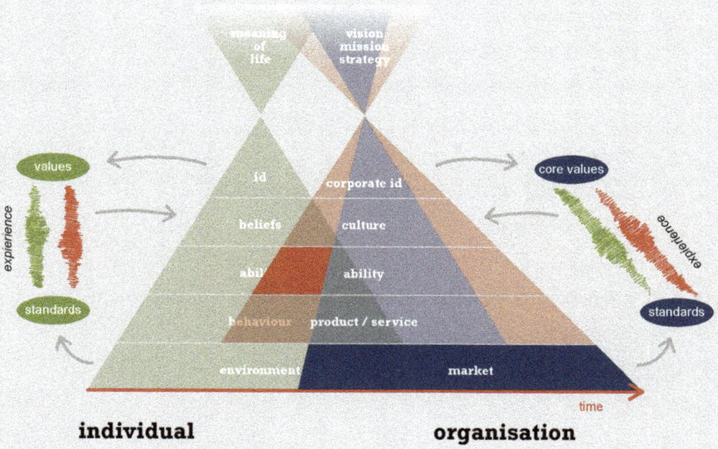

Roy is taking a radical decision, based on the right information. Knowing that disposing of this product has direct consequences for RTech's capital. For the machinery as well as for the human capital. Together they form the company's capital, even though the machines are classified in the balance sheet, while the human capital more often is not. Even though machines are classified as assets and employees as an expense. Firing people often is an evident solution, because it cuts costs and it does not have a negative influence on the assets in the balance sheet.

So it is in fact true that, from an accounting perspective, cuts made in human capital do not have a negative influence on your capital. But what is an employees' worth? Considering all their knowledge and experience, their education and motivation? And how much do machines cost when they are not operating? Insurances to cover this capital? And company buildings merely kept on for storage?

Finally, we see that there is still a reason for RTech to exist. The blue pyramid has become smaller, but there still is a customer base that can create a positive result after a reorganisation. Because when the fire has been put out, there is still an overlap between the level of products and services and the market level. The products and services that RTech delivers to other customers are sold with profit. When looking at what you do have, you can start developing from that point onwards.

> *'Forget about all the reasons why something may not work. You only need to find one good reason why it will.'*
> ***Robert Anthony***

Reflection

Answer the following questions to look at the ability of your organisation to deal with large fluctuations in demand.

1	Machines are not utilised to maximum capacity	Yes / No
2	Employees work hard, but sickness absence is below average	Yes / No
3	If demand drops to half of the current demand, I can easily switch to another product	Yes / No
4	If demand drops to half of the current demand, employees can easily switch to another production line	Yes / No
5	A swift growth of 30% can easily be dealt with by both machines as well as employees	Yes / No

If you answered Yes three times or more, it might be useful to consider how to make your company more flexible.

We are not moving? That sounds like music to my ears. It also sounds logical to me. If you calculate the costs of having to move all those heavy machines to another company building. The transportation costs. Not to mention the risks of damage. I have good insurance, but damages resulting from transportation are not covered. No, moving is not an option. Thank god. But still, I am afraid that we are going to have to shut down many of the machines. And this means the costs would be higher than the revenues. So, I would have to sell them. Do I really need to get rid of them? Really need to sell them? Those machines still have so much potential! Am I really forced to hand over this gold to the competition? Just to add a few pounds to my account? An amount so disproportionate to the money I would be making if those machines were up and running and making beautiful products like they are supposed to. When I close my eyes, I can still see them creating the most fantastic products. Not just the products our customers knew, but also the innovative ones that more often were even better. But I am going to have to be patient, because now isn't the right time. But I do not want to sell them either. We could temporarily put some machines to work, after some technical adaptations, on other products. So they would at least make up for the downtime costs. That sounds like a great idea to me. Cutting costs and maybe even somewhat covering some costs. Max agrees that it is a good idea, as long as it fits a broader vision of the future!

When everything appears to be turning out all right, Max mentions my staff. This comes as a surprise to me, because he knows we have already tackled that issue and I am not about to fire any more people. Enough is enough. We have got our heads above the water again, so now we are just going to keep on swimming. Still Max won't let go of the issue. He is talking about safety issues in the organisation, but security is one of the most important process indicators to a high-tech company like mine. Security has top priority. So assuming that it would be unsafe is complete nonsense. But still, a few days later, after several conversations with many of my staff, I am starting to see what Max is getting at.

It seems I am not the type of person they can open up to. While I was under the impression that I have a very outgoing and trustworthy appearance… I am broad-minded and flexible. A true leader according to the many large management books that fill my book shelves. What more do they want? They have not actually said it, but their behaviour makes it all the more obvious. Their attitude, lack of openness, distance. I dared to ask a few people straight out. Hesitantly, but without any doubt I just asked. I am not just the owner, inventor or founder of this company. To my people, I am their boss. Their manager. Their supervisor. And just like it is far more easy to tell a friend that you are having problems at work than it is telling your wife, it is more difficult for employees to open up to their boss. Especially after the hard times we are now trying to leave behind, in which we were forced to let go many of their colleagues. Everybody is scared to admit that they are troubled or just not happy in their current position. They too have an entrenched fear of losing their own jobs.

How do I deal with this? They do not confide in me about everything. They do make that very clear to me. But if they do not confide in me, who will they confide in? Who can they turn to with their problems, with their struggles? If I am not aware of things going wrong, how will I be able to intervene?

I realise now more than ever, just how crucial it is to keep my people motivated. To guide them through the changed, or in fact still changing, organisation. To show them how to deal with their new roles. I cannot ignore it any longer; I will have to invest in the company culture, no matter how senseless it might have sounded to me at first.

But what is all this going to cost? If I cannot solve this from the inside, I will have to look for an external party, screen them, not to mention pay them. I am just beginning to get the cash flows back on track again. I am not looking for another huge expense. It was all about saving money, wasn't it? Max responds calmly but firmly: 'Does this not mean that you will have to be careful with what you have left?'

> *Director to HR-manager: 'What if we invest in our people and then they leave?' HR-manager: 'What if we do not and they stay?'*
> ***Berthold Gunster | Flip-thinking***

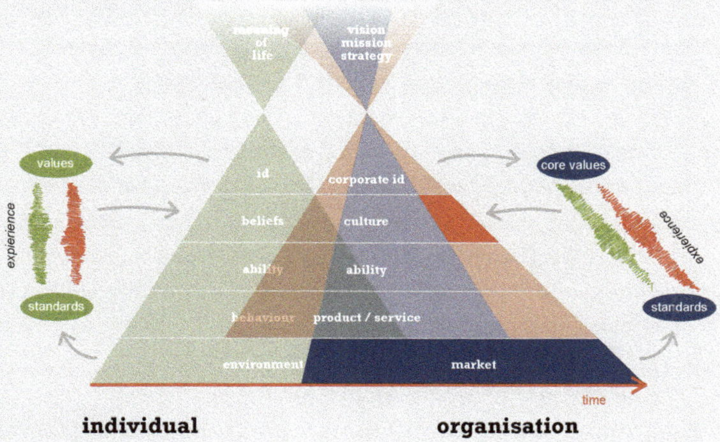

What is happening?

The standards have shifted due to changing market conditions. RTech's values no longer suit the markets' norm. This leads to a substantial negative experience, directly affecting the organisations' culture. The belief 'together we are winners' turns into a culture of 'we will have to adjust to the situation and see from there.' How this affects motivation and performance does not require any further explanation.

At the level of Roy's role (overlap green and blue) we see tension between the individuals' beliefs and the organisations' new culture. In order to go with the flow of the market, it is crucial to start investing in the organisational culture. It is no coincidence that RTech lost the customer. That was because the company did not move along with the market's standards. RTech has been a production company for years, producing high tech products because it could. Quality always came first. Now they are on the verge of becoming a market-oriented organisation that produces leading products that match the demand.

At the same time, some kind of role play is going on. Everybody takes on a different role in the company. Similarly, people play several roles among family and friends. In fact, you take on a different role in each environment. Which role you are going to play is not just determined by your environment, but also by your abilities and of course, your beliefs. And these can be very conflicting factors. If I am convinced of the fact that I am a good manager while in fact I am not, I won't be granted a managerial role. At least, not for long. As it is proven to be as counterproductive to fulfil a function for which you are not qualified, it is just as counterproductive to not be awarded such a function when you are qualified.

Roy had the belief that his employees trusted him with everything and now he is experiencing that apparently this was not the case. This is caused by Roy's role in the organisation. The director role is a different role than the best friend role. A director who has just had to fire half of his staff, probably will be looked at in a different way than before.

Reflection

How many roles do you have in your organisation? And in your family?

Do you experience tensions between those roles? Do they expect you to effectively perform two roles, which cannot be accomplished at the same time? Tensions between your work and private time? Tensions between different roles at your work?

Since there are often tensions between your roles, we advise you to talk about it to someone who can give you insights in your roles and the expectations that result from them. No one has ever died from working hard. People die because of the high level of stress that they experience when performing multiple conflicting roles.

Who can help me and will contribute to the profit of the company, rather than be a liability? I can still hear Max saying to me: How much do anxious sales managers cost you when they do not win the contracts? How much do anxious employees cost when they make unnecessary mistakes? And: how much will it cost you if you do not invest in it? By now I get the point, but how, who, where? Even before my hands touch my hair, I notice a blog from a change manager on my social media. Shared by one of my contacts. It immediately draws my attention.

It is all about HOW

As a manager, we are always dealing with results. We manage the processes and the people and we want nothing more than for all the Key Performance Indicators to say we are on target. So the big question is... how are we going to improve the results? Are we going to take on the same amount of work with less people? Or maybe even more work? How can we update our processes? Can we do something quicker, easier or more efficiently? This management style is called the HOW-style.

The result is usually a bit disappointing. We start working harder, putting in more hours just to turn the KPIs to green. Unfortunately, we do not realise that a KPI merely records the things we did yesterday: yesterday our production level was 56%. Last year the revenue per customer was 6% lower.

So, when we look at the KPIs, we are actually looking at the past! This is practical and easy, because it allows us to pinpoint why we did or did not achieve certain goals. When times get tough, this will only cause demotivation. Because we work hard every day to make progress, though we get stuck in the results from our past.

Relying only on KPI's won't lead to sustainable improvement. For that you will need something more focussed on the future. A good intention? A different approach towards the client? Another perspective?

And then there is the HOW-question. How are we going to make sure we will perform better tomorrow than we did today? Immediately the impact of human behaviour needs to be evaluated. If we change our behaviour, we will get different results. HOW-questions provide us with insight: how are we going to make sure that we will know exactly what to do differently tomorrow? How are we going to implement that? How are we going to make sure that we do not relapse in old behaviour? How are we doing at the moment? How do other companies approach this? And how could we implement that approach into our organisation?

To me, management is all about the HOW-questions. How to improve the current behaviour of the employees, so tomorrow's results will be better than today's. In short... it is all about the HOW.

Ty Johnson

Without any hesitation, I pick up the phone. I do not have to negotiate with Max just to make sure I got it right. To make sure I am doing the right thing. I call Ty and a few days later he is sitting at my heavy, dark conference table. Ty studied business economics at one point. After that he got a master in something like human behaviour, because he wanted to know why some people are successful while others are not. Finally, he started a company in organisational development. "To bring a company from A to B, not by typing a report on how it can be done, but by showing the people in the company that they are able to do it", he says. Ty believes in people's natural power to change, especially when those powers are combined and focussed on a goal. That is the only way to change a company and have sustainable impact, according to him.

Unlike my first conversation with Max at this very same table, I now know exactly how to express my reason for calling him. What I expect from him. Powerful, to the point, persuasive. I want trust to be rebuilt within RTech. I want my people to go through the changes that the company is going through, so they will embrace them. I want to connect with the future. Never having to experience all the things that have happened these past few weeks ever again. Be futureproof! Create a culture that is free of such misery. Ty is nodding and his story confirms once more that calling him has been the right thing to do. When Ty lets me in on the core values of his company, I am fully convinced of this match and I cannot wait for us to get started.

Trust | Connect | Improve

Finally, after all these months of living with the secret of my company going down, I am not scared to talk about it anymore. Now we are all starting to recharge, I am no longer scared to share all the things that have happened to me. The responses I receive from my environment take me by surprise. To me it felt like failing when I realised that I wouldn't make it without external help. However, people around me called this effective leadership. As it turns out, knowing who to call for help when times get rough within your organisation is a considered choice, not a failure. Now I do not want to take all the credit, because after all, I am the one who put my company in a compromising position. But it was in fact me who took action. A bit late, but I still called for help. Just in time, because I did not have all the answers myself. Just in time, I accepted the fact that I needed someone else's expertise in order to survive.

Of course Ty also had to listen to my story, since he is the one who has to determine what our starting point will be. He seems to be a powerful and competent man, who knows what he is talking about. Not just because this is his field of study, but because he has seen this happening to a number of organisations before. He has been asked to intervene many times. The big names referred to on his website do not impress me enough to trust his entire story. But he radiates tranquillity, just like Max. Tranquillity based on experience and expertise. Based on trust. And Ty isn't shocked by my story either. The fact that I have turned to Max for help is what he considers to be a sign of strength. Asking for help is not a sign of weakness. I had actually shown true leadership by asking experts for help.

We arrange a follow-up appointment so we can make some concrete plans. So, we can take action. Move forward. I have my organisational chart within reach, as well as all the information we could possibly be needing. I have put a huge pile of paper and a large number of dark blue folders in front of me on the oakwood. It is just a table, but I am still so attached to its' heaviness. It always feels like its' solid character adds weight to the room and the conversation. I am full of hope and expectation as I sit down right where I'd already put my notebook. The first sheet is already filled with a clear overview of today's topics. Ty is sitting right in front of me and, just like me, he has a beautiful leather folder. It contains a notebook, pen and an iPad. During our conversation, he frequently uses it as a reference, but mostly to explain things with graphic representations. During this second appointment, it becomes clear that I want to start off way too fast.

I had prepared myself for one or a few action plans regarding my human capital. The organisational culture, which is now uncertain and, as a consequence, destabilises the people and therefore the company. I can imagine the scene: Ty having conversations with my people at all levels of my company. Bringing them closer together, so trust can be built and motivation increases. The easing of the production processes is nothing more than a logical consequence. Customers simply won't be able to stay away, so RTech will blossom and become even more successful than it had ever been. All because of its' motivated employees.

Yet Ty wants to go in a completely different direction. After having heard my vision on this conversation and the period ahead, he first wants to talk to me about the upcoming changes in my role. The role I want to play in my future organisation. And he wants to talk about my responsibilities.

'A change manager is responsible for the steps during the process, not for the content. If you keep doing the same things you did 2 years ago, how will you make sure the results will be different this time?'

> *Insanity:*
> *Doing the same things over and over again and expecting different results.*
> ***Albert Einstein***

I am both confused and hurt, as I am trying to take it all in. We decide to continue the appointment tomorrow and I use the rest of the time I had scheduled for this conversation to get some fresh air. When I walk through the front door of the building, the strong wind slaps me in the face. But I defy the harsh autumn weather and I realise I do not do this as often as I should. Distance myself and look at my company from an entirely different point of view. For months and years now, I have only been looking at the white concrete interior of the building. But when you look at the outside, all that is left of it is a faint impression of what once was a building painted in stylish blue. Time hasn't been kind to the beautiful exterior. The paint is peeling and the walls are now covered with various plants, which have lost their green colour and their leaves because of this chilly time of year. After a 45 minute walk, I suddenly find myself right in front of Max' house. When I tell him that I really need to start painting next weekend and I would also like to cut the hedge, Max says:

'How are you going to take responsibility when you do not even have a clue what your responsibilities in your role are?'

This rather confronting question suddenly makes me realise the point that Ty was trying to make. Of course, it is my responsibility to make sure that my company has the right look. From the inside as well as from the outside. It might be my responsibility to choose the colour. But it is definitely not my responsibility to actually paint the building. In other words, I have to let it go.

Max points out that, although I have a hard time handing over responsibility to others, I have absolutely no problem handing over the responsibility of making the necessary changes that RTech is going to have to deal with, to Ty and Max. Is that because of my fear of failure? To let people down? Let myself down? Fear for the unknown? For the future, of what the future appears to be, when you look at it from the thin thread on which I am now trying to keep my balance?

'Fear, the worst of all enemies,
cab be effectively cured
by forced repetition
of acts of courage'
Napoleon Hill

'Have faith', Max says. We are going to work on that the coming period. I am in fact one of the employees of the company. I am also part of the organisational culture. I will also have to change so the company will be able to go with the flow of the changing market. That is evident. Max always manages to firmly put my feet back on the ground again. I totally get it; When I work on my personal development, I am also working to improve the company. Because my company and I are inextricably linked. Yet this is the point where Max intervenes.

> *'Roy you are not your company. You fulfil a role within your company. If you work on yourself, you will become more objective towards your company and that will make it easier for you to let things go. If you take a step back, you will be able to see the bigger picture. Creating distance is not about letting go of responsibilities. It is about taking your own responsibility and showing leadership. It is not about letting go and just see what happens. Creating distance provides a connected helicopter view.'*

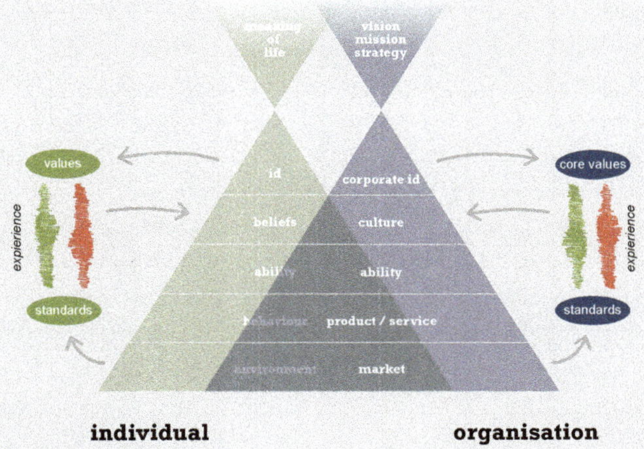

What is happening?

Ty clarifies the different roles which Max and Ty fulfil with the the Z-model of Change®.

Max is focused on Roy's personal development. His Change Perspective starts on the left side of the model, looking towards the right side. He is primarily looking at Roy, the individual (the green pyramid in the model). His conversations focus on Roy as a person. He also talks about Roy's role within and as part of the organisation (where green and blue overlap in the model). Max' role is one of personal executive coaching on personal beliefs.

Ty is focussed on the development of the organisation (the blue pyramid in the model). His change perspective starts on the right side of the model, looking towards the left. His main focus is on the organisation, followed by the roles of individuals like Roy. Ty's role is one of business change consultant.

Of course, Roy is part of that (the overlap), but Ty only addresses his role as the director of RTech. Furthermore, Ty is focussed on the functional roles of all the employees, the overlap between organisation (blue) and individual (green). Ty only focusses on the person behind the role to enable him to identify any beliefs that might block progress and to give the right personal support when that happens. As blocking beliefs result in people not being able to function properly within a company.

In that case, you need to find another personal coach, another Max, to ensure the situation remains safe for the employee. Of course, the effect of the personal coaching will be visible in the performance of one's role within the company, which will be noticeable by the employees, Ty (and Roy) and all other people around him.

The overlap between individual and organisation is the overlap between Max' and Ty's role. But only where Roy's role within the organisation is concerned. Primarily it is Roy who notices this overlap and any differences in the way Max and Ty approach issues in this area. This means it is up to him to talk about this with either Max or Ty. In general, Roy will discuss his personal questions with Max and will talk to Ty about the organisational development.

Reflection

Previously we talked about your roles and the tensions you can experience between them. It is good to think about the roles you want to fulfil in someone else's life.

As a manager, would you fulfil the role of a coach? Or is it possible that these are conflicting roles. Would you like to be the coach of a co-worker, meaning you must directly report on a close colleague? Under what conditions would that be possible? If it is even possible at all?

As friends, do you want to do business together? Or is it better to go on a walk with friends rather than to trade with friends. It would be a great idea to discuss your boundaries regarding this subject with some people around you. Food for thought.

4 Mind shift

Once every two weeks I have an appointment with Max, which mainly consists of me asking him many questions and him answering as little of them as possible. But still I feel that these meetings are invaluable to me. I notice Max helps me to straighten out my thoughts, so I come up with all the answers myself. Most of the time it does take a while before the penny drops. Or rather, before all the pieces of the puzzle fall into place. Every time Max manages to organise my thoughts and recognise my strategies. For example, why I did not take action, did not decide, did not listen, acted like an ostrich, did not believe my employees and so on. I now know what drives me, what strategies I use and why sometimes they work and sometimes they do not. And because I see why they do not work, I am prepared to change those strategies into strategies that probably will work. Once those old strategies were appropriate, and once they had worked. But that is no guarantee for the future. I can choose my behaviour and am aware of my new insights. It feels like freedom, tranquillity and wisdom. That is an eye-opening experience, because just a few months ago I thought I knew everything.

I cannot envision myself as a person without my company. And vice versa. This is one of the things Max has tried to point out to me in a subtle way over and over again. He helps me see the person inside me, the person I am unable to see for myself. Max stimulates me in figuring things out for myself according to the role I am playing at that time. And whether or not this contributes to the situation or just to my ego. Painful, yet essential.

Lencioni, that is the model he showed me and the book he gave me to read. This model clearly illustrates the dance between my ego and the results of my company. Using this model, Max intervenes every time he feels I am taking a decision for myself instead of for my business. And this is slightly confrontational, I can tell you that. Yet I do feel this is a positive thing. I had absolutely no idea that my ego could play up like this. Even though this appears to be human. So, it is only for the best and also important that I am aware of this now. Because this means that from now on, I can consciously take business decisions, which are purely in the interest of RTech. After all, if RTech is doing well, I am doing well business wise. Max likes to refer to this as 'a strategic reorganisation of personal priorities'. I just refer to this as intense, yet revealing.

In the middle of difficulty
lies opportunity
Albert Einstein

I am not the only one doing everything he can to get this company back on track again. My sales manager Ann, 32, married and ambitious, does the same. She warned me time and time again, but I did not listen. I couldn't listen, because I was working too hard. Ann developed herself into a true leader who works hard to get things under control. Together with the account managers, she has made special offers based on the extra production Peter can take on with his swiftly converted machines. The goal is to let them make swifter decisions, and to increase turnover. The account managers have approached new clients with a special offer. A number of them have accepted the offer. It's their initial introduction to RTech, and it is much-needed revenue for us. For our existing clients, appointments have been made and projects have been started, to improve our current products and even to develop some new products. All within the present possibilities of course.

At procurement we have done our utmost to negotiate the best terms of payment with our suppliers. That helped a lot. And of course, we informed the bank. They are not really helping at the moment, but we are in good contact and they might be willing to help us out on occasion.

The resignation of half our staff, together with the sales of machinery, the temporary conversion of other machines to produce products that sell better and the switching off of the money tap has resulted in a clear view of our losses. These are no longer critical. Everyone is working really hard, but our actions have led to our company no longer being in danger of folding. We can survive on the cash flow now. Not that we can survive for years, but for now it is the best we can do.

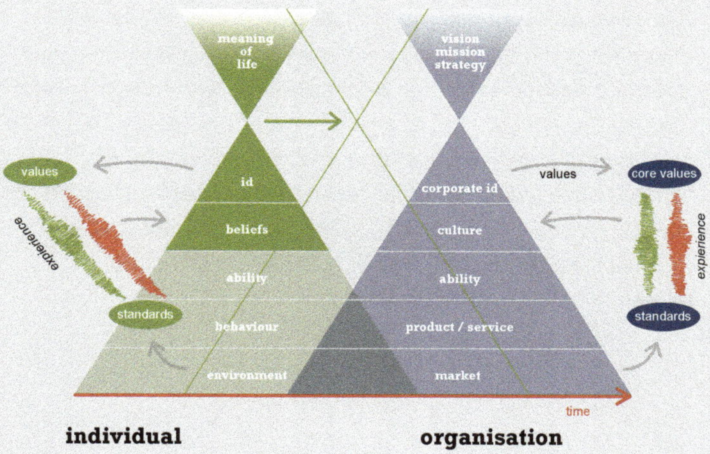

What is happening?

Since RTech is on the move and Roy is in charge, he is in the unfortunate position to encounter his own beliefs which are blocking his progress. Roy has a role to play. As a director during a time of crisis. And he has absolutely no experience with that. His old beliefs, not just on a personal level but on a commercial level as well, have enabled him to get to the point where he is now. And that is still not the desired situation. Max continuously talks to Roy about Roy's personal beliefs. He consistently gives Roy feedback at times when Roy puts his personal interests above the company interests. This way it is made clear to Roy that his personal identity is different from his role in the organisation. And different from the identity of his company.

Roy discovers that he actually does not really know what is most important to him in his personal life. His personal values are unknown to him. He wants to go through this personal process together with Max, so he can gain self-knowledge on his personal motivations.

This book however, primarily focuses on the organisational development. Roy's development in personal leadership will nevertheless become visible in his behaviour (in the role he plays).

Reflection

Everyone experiences things that are important for his or her life. We can cherish those moments, although they are not necessarily positive. We can even cherish the negative experiences, because they give us insight into who we are. They show us the moments when our personal values collided with the standards of our environment.

For example, when someone gets fired multiple times, he can learn that his personal value "freedom" is at odds with the standards of his manager, who wants employees to act exactly the way he expects them to. Although the firing process is not a fun experience, he can learn what his personal values are. This will help him to avoid a similar situation and search for an environment in which freedom to make your own choices is more appreciated.

It is smart to think about your own personal values. Just write down a few important experiences and think about what you can learn from them. What do these experiences say about you? Why was there a conflict? Or, why did that particular experience make you happy?

5 Teambuilding

Extinguish, mop, build. Building. Finally! It thought we would never get to this point. Not so long ago, I was standing at the foot of a huge mountain. No point in climbing it. Many pathways destroyed by the storm. Not enough Sherpas to set out new pathways. It just seemed like an impossible task. After I received help from various parties, I was able to look at the mountain from a different point of view and it appeared to be a lot smaller. I was able to divide the mountain into several smaller hills. Those were easier to pass. Easier to overview. I surrounded myself with the right people to help me and together we decided which would be the right pathway to take. With combined knowledge. Combined forces. A combined wealth of experience. We will all be sharing an extra special part of that wealth in due time. I am ready for the climb, although I realise it won't always be easy. I am ready for the many walks up the pathways which are also part of the journey and which won't be as hard as I had feared. Many new people will come my way. To share both short and longer, positive and negative experiences with.

Building. Finally. A renewed company, which is not completely disconnected from the old one. Building and letting go of the old that is keeping us old. Building the road that leads to future sustainability. That leads to stable, solid, continuous profitability. Building the people who are getting ready to come along. Building. Both the foundation as well as the windows, which enable us to look outside. Both the supporting walls as well as the beautifully shaped partition walls. Both the full-automatic air circulation system, as well as the indispensable fresh air supply. After a long period of deconstructing and licking wounds, we are finally ready to start building.

Ty is the one who will be defining and guarding the process, since he is a lot more experienced at it than I am. I am responsible for the content, because after all, RTech is my company.

But I am not used to playing this role. How are we going to do this? How will I know how to deal with this, when I am unaware of the content?

But these thoughts are, not coincidentally, the purpose of the first step we are taking in this process. So this is not the time to sit back and relax, but to make plans straight away. Action. I love it. Yet again, the reality is different than I'd expected. Ty proposes that I don't determine the content on my own, but to do that together with my department managers. He asks me whether all the responsibilities had weighed heavily on me. Doing it all by myself all these years. If I hadn't felt lonely while making all those decisions on my own. But I had never thought about it that way. Could my biggest client leaving me be interpreted as a sign that it was time to go for a more futureproof way of organising. Uhhm.

'Wasn't it lonely at the top?'

For years now I have been the one to determine the vision. I have been translating it into company goals and communicating these throughout the organisation. To Ann, my sales manager. To Peter, my production manager of 14 years, better known as a technical genius instead of a manager. To Bill, my financial manager who is loyal and reliable. And to Richard, my logistics manager, who is highly energetic in getting the products to the customers. It is their job to realize this vision.

Top-down Ty calls it, and I am in no position to say that this has been a success. I can only agree that indeed, as of now, we have got to do things differently. More effectively. More solid and moreover, carried by the most important company asset: the people. A different way of organising it is then. Not handing over responsibilities to others, but sharing responsibilities. Not instructing, but inspiring. Not forcing, but motivating. Making use of one's knowledge, qualities, insights, points of view. Together we know more. I am all for it. But it certainly is a huge transition for both my managers as for myself.

During my private conversations with Max I more frequently come to the conclusion that my management team has some very useful views which complement my view of RTech and its' environment. Together we gradually conclude that my faith in them is growing. And by now I also acknowledge that my managers deserve no less than that. Sometimes I wonder why I have not noticed that before. Why I have not given them the chance before.

> *There are only two days a year*
> *that nothing can be done.*
> *One is called Yesterday and the other*
> *is called Tomorrow.*
> *Today is the right day to Love, Believe,*
> *Do and mostly Live.*
> ***Dalai Lama***

All of my managers are attending our recently initiated fortnightly MT meeting, in which every department is represented. In which every manager informs us on the ins and outs of his or her department. In which we discuss the points for improvement and the blind spots. In which we are honest about the positives and the negatives. In which I inform them on the developments in securing the business' future and business renewal. This way I am inviting them to get involved in creating a future for RTech. A joint future, which is supported by the MT. Commitment that will be noticeable throughout the entire organisation. But no matter how logical and hopeful Ty's plan sounds, I have absolutely no idea whether they are ready for this. Whether I am ready for this. No idea whether they are capable. Whether I am capable. What do they know about running a business? Isn't that supposed to be my role? After all, it is my company.

'It is your company, as well as theirs.
They are your co-employees'.

Max. I talked to Max last week about the fact that I am taking it all quite personally. That I have got the feeling that I have failed. That I am not good enough. That I am just not capable of being a director. It is not a very comforting thought that, according to Max, this is just a logical response when you are in the middle of a company crisis. It does not make me struggle with these feelings any less. Asking me to hand over my company when it is most vulnerable, when it needs me most. It does not sound like a logical response to a company crisis. That sounds like a failing leader. Incomprehensible, to put the source of income of over two hundred employees in the hands of people who are not used to playing the leading part. Who, as a matter of fact, have absolutely no interest in taking on such responsibilities on top of their regular duties.

'Why have you got this all figured out for them? Have you asked them? Why are we even talking about your employees? You feel like you are failing as a leader. That is got nothing to do with the wishes and abilities of your department managers.

What am I supposed to say now? Yes, I do feel like I have failed. Why cannot I be the one to rescue the company I have built? Why cannot I breathe new life into it? I have built this company from scratch. I have lead it all the way to the top. How does Ty have the nerve to say that I am not allowed to do that again?

'Is that what he is saying?'

No, Max. Not in those words. Of course not. But I do have to hand over responsibility. Partially. I have to share it. With those who are merely used to leading a department, not an entire company. Which of course isn't a small task, but it isn't quite the same thing either.

'What would happen if you would involve them?'

I do not know. Nobody knows. So, the only option for me now, is to give an affirmative answer to the question whether or not I am prepared to give them a chance, whether or not I am willing to let them surprise me.

Back at the table for the MT meeting, Ty was present in the background. This way he could identify opportunities and, if need may be, make adjustments in the form of reflection towards me in one of our personal conversations. I tell my MT in a clear and professional manner about the concept of shared responsibility and about the necessity to bring RTech to a steady level. A level that will enable us to joyfully work on our quality products that meet our customers' needs. Naturally, I end my monologue by asking them if they like the idea to co-build this new RTech. Fortunately, I only get positive responses from everyone at the table. Ann, energetic and positive as always, shares that she sees opportunities in the market. Bill acts a bit worried and says that we really must pay close attention to the costs. Richard nods and places the remark that he has to deal with some resource problems, but that he will be able to manage that. And Peter just goes along with the rest. We decide to organise a strategic session to make the blueprint for RTech 2.0. This should be led by Ty and held somewhere off-site. And while Ty is enthusiastic about the first impression, I cannot wait to share my experiences with Max.

Ty's questions, which I had left unanswered, are taking hold of me. Unfortunately, Max only adds to this feeling by asking me what would happen if Ty is right. Do I trust my people? Have I ever given them my trust?

Trusting others is something you gain by giving it away.
Martijn de Zoete

You see, I have failed. Just as I was regaining my self-confidence… Max on the other hand, thinks differently and is able to redefine and give me some hope.

> *'You only fail when you consciously do something differently from what you know to be best . Denying the real situation is an unconscious survival response which is quite normal, because the consequences of reality are bigger than you think you can handle. However, you will eventually be confronted with reality, which will enable you to see how strong you really are.*
>
> *Remember, not making a choice is also a choice, only then the choice will be made for you… Only too often a crisis proves that you are stronger, wiser and better than you had imagined before.'*

Our days off site are approaching. It is only after my conversation with Max that I am actually able to give my MT the active role Ty told me to give them. The purpose of our days off site is threefold, he explains. We will be looking for a clear framework for a renewed vision on RTech. We are going to get a clearer picture of the MT members. And by 'we' I do not just refer to Ty and I, but also to the MT members themselves. And they will be getting a clearer picture of me, so I'll have to come clean as well. Scary, but at the same time it will bring us insight, be inspiring and bring us closer together. Ty is full of questions. What is everyone's personal motivation? What image do they have on their role in the organisation? And what will the possible differences be between their personal values and their current (old) and new role?

After that, and just as important, building trust between the team members and between the MT and myself, as a director. This way we will be working on a healthier organisational culture at the same time.

The purpose of our days off site has been communicated internally and it is causing a lot of commotion among many employees. Particularly the expectation that an active role will be required from the department managers during the relaunch of the company. Both employees as well as managers are dealing with emotions ranging from shock, fear and anxiety to hope. Fortunately, the latter prevails and a week later all six of us head out to the spend two days on a sailing boat at sea. Sleeping in pairs in a berth onboard a ship will work out just fine. But we also have to navigate a ship. And there is nobody around to define the roles. At least, it won't be me. Before going on this trip, I received a clear message from Ty not to do anything but observe. Not to take on the leading role, as everyone is expecting from me. As I am used to take on.

> *'What will happen when you let them take the responsibility? Do you trust them?'*

> *'How much space, freedom and responsibility are you able to give them? In other words: do you really trust them?'*

Uncomfortable. I tell them I trust them, but I realise that I have never actually shown my trust in them. I cannot let go without trust. Letting go isn't easy. I cannot just say 'I cannot do this'. Letting go is a choice, Ty explains. It is a conscious decision to change something. To do something different than you did yesterday. But when you are used to holding on, he continues, when you are used to clinging on to something, the step towards relaxation will initially be painful. And it will be painful. Still, I understand that first I have to let go of something before anyone else can catch it. This means I will have to have faith that someone else will catch it.

I understand the thought and keep repeating this to myself while we are embarking. To my managers, it will be a clear signal that they will have to take on an active role to keep the ship on course. But just like the huge mountain that controlled my mind at first, I cannot find a suitable rope nor a large number of Sherpas who've had years of experience in doing this. Surprisingly enough, defining the roles runs smoothly and in no time, everyone has found his place on board of the sailing boat. During our two-day sailing trip this is not the only welcome surprise shown by my people. Despite, or should I say thanks to the unexpected bad weather conditions. Because as soon as the bad weather sets in...

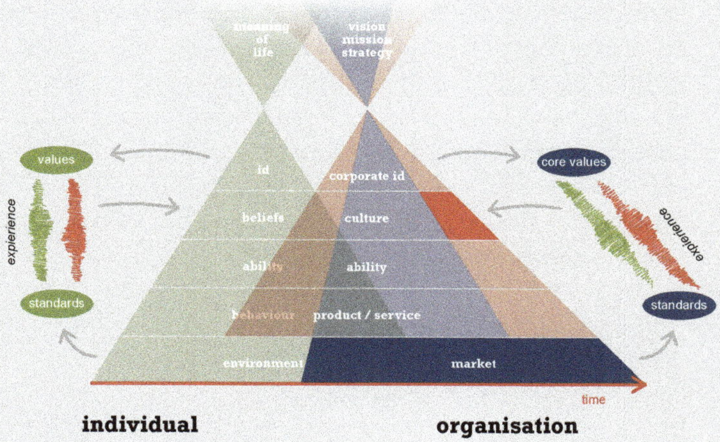

What is happening?

People feel safer to discover new qualities and competences within themselves and within colleagues, when they are taken away from their daily working environment. Sailing and sleeping together on a ship builds trust and makes people bond. The roles of captain, navigator, chief mate, sailor and cook are great metaphors for the working environment.

On board the MT is building a new RTech culture. A futureproof culture. One that is not operated top-down, but one in which every individual is aware of his own responsibility. Where there is trust in colleagues, resulting in a working environment based on equality.

> *Equality respects the uniqueness of an individual and his role. The presumption is that all individuals are different and are therefore valued as equals. When a manager communicates with his employees on the basis of equality, he will balance the relationship, without forgoing his role as a manager.*
> ***Martijn de Zoete | AnyChange***

Reflection

How aware are you of your own organisation's culture, or is it something you just do not think about? Working hard is nice, but then you are only considering the level of abilities. Working hard is like a motor with a lot of horsepower. That has a lot of abilities too, to accelerate. Questions like "how do we do the things we do?" or "How do we work together?", are questions concerning the culture of the organisation.

There are organisation cultures where yelling at each other is considered to be normal, instead of talking with a normal tone of voice. There are cultures where the manager or supervisor does all the thinking and the employees do not think for themselves at all. There are cultures where gossip is the standard, instead of giving feedback. But, luckily, there are cultures in which people talk on a normal level and conflicts are being addressed with a helicopter view.

It is wise to think about your organisation's culture. When you can bring those thoughts back to three or five words, you have defined the actual core values. Two words? That is not enough. Six words? Too much. Three to five.

When you can't change the direction of the wind. Adjust your sails.
H. Jackson Brown

We switch roles every few hours. Change positions on the ship. Surprisingly insightful. I am not only surprised by my own people, but also by my own adaptability. Switching from captain to navigator is an acceptable transition. I know exactly which way to go and the new first mate follows my instructions effortlessly. Up until the point when we have a group evaluation and Ty asks us to step out of our comfort zone. He asks us to take on a completely different role than the one that we are used to at RTech. To surprise and discover ourselves and the others.

Even though I had seen this, absolutely not optional, request coming, I cannot say it sounds appealing. Even though I was prepared for a surprising effect, the impact it has on me is neither surprising nor positive. The sailor jacket is too tight and the deck around the captain's cabin is now spotless, since I am afraid to leave the fire out of sight for too long. Letting go is easier said than done. Being forced to hand over the helm of the ship does not mean I want to witness someone else navigating the ship. Dependency. My biggest fear. Handing over the ship triggers this feeling of being dependent. I had chosen to become an entrepreneur just so I would be independent.

But overall it is going quite nicely. I have not been on the fore side of the deck. But from the aft deck, near the first mate, I can see exactly what everybody is doing. Is everything going as it should and are there no irregularities? I am in a central position, so everyone can address me when needed. But to my surprise there is no need for that. It is all running smoothly. The boat is on a steady course and during our moment of reflection later on, it turns out that others share my point of view. Despite my own dissatisfying temporary role as a sailor in this entire scenario, it is nice to see and hear that everyone is so positive. To sit here, Ty and I, together with my sales, production, logistics and finance managers. Once these were four different worlds, led by me from my overarching individual world. And now we are at sea, in between those different worlds and the roles we play within RTech are no longer important. Because now we are one. One world.

I can only say that I am pleasantly surprised. Not just by the sense of togetherness and the way all things seem to come together here on this boat. I also see qualities and competences I have never seen in my people. That is quite an eye-opener. You see many of them grow. Confidence, and also cooperation I did not think was possible up until now. Ty listens more than he speaks, but there is not a moment of silence. Everyone has a story to share. Mostly about positive adventures and surprising experiences. Complimenting one another. There is room for positivity and candour. Ty does not seem surprised, but satisfied, when he concludes towards everyone, but toward me in particular:

> *'When trust is given, possibilities are rewarded.'*

Of course, not everyone is as enthusiastic. But in general, this had been a successful day, better than I could have imagined. Peter did not seem to have experienced the trust as much as the rest of us, but maybe that is just my imagination. After all, not everyone expresses their feelings the same way. Must be my imagination. It had been a long day. We have another drink in the galley and then prepare to hit the sack.

The second day starts off really well and it does not take long before I am the one responsible to serve a hot meal during lunch. I have to get used to not being on deck, but down in the galley, far away from all the action. But I let it all happen. Yesterday I had built up some confidence in my people. I have seen what they are capable of. I have seen that the ship continues to sail even though I am not the one in control. I am now in control of the sausages and potatoes. And as far as I am concerned, this is an important role as well. After all, you cannot function without a decent meal. To me, this has also been an extremely valuable sailing trip, because it has forced me to change my perspective. More than once a day. It is a lot to handle, but it has given me a wealth of experience. The importance of so-called subordinate roles. Their indispensability. And the creativity people develop whenever they are given the space to do so. An unforgettable journey as far as I am concerned.

I had just about settled in, after having spent an entire day clenching my teeth so I could hand over the helm. Let Ty set the course. But then he handed it over to the department managers. Who weren't quite used to this. Which made me want to offer them my help. I wanted to guide them. Through a situation that was entirely new to all of us. I was finally able to let go of my directing role and limit myself to only keeping an eye on things from a distance, and then the weather changed. Yesterday was an autumnal sailing day with a nice strong wind, a soft drizzle and a bit of sun. Today, the weather is severe. Heavy gusts of wind, hailstorms and nothing but dark thunder clouds. I do not just notice this by the noise, but also by the fact that the boat has suddenly changed course. This is not a good thing. Even though I am assigned to be the cook for this part of the day, I drop everything. The potatoes no longer have the status of being the essential fuel and are now rolling across the floor, while I run up to the deck as fast as I can. Lunch will have to wait. There are more important things to do now. Right now.

But just as I am about to take over the helm, Ty intervenes. For the first time since we got on this boat. But he does not get it. This is an emergency. There is no time for playing games at sea right now. There are more important things at stake right now.

'More important than trusting your management team?'

He does not seem to realise the fact that this is an emergency, something we did not take into account, that we did not prepare for, nor the fact that we have not got time to play games. He keeps asking me this question three, four, five times. Until I finally know where I stand. At this moment, on this boat, I am the cook.

But… the panic on deck hits me even harder when I am on my way back to the galley and the only thing I can do is watch helplessly. It is probably a good thing that I am being forced to stay below deck in the galley of the unsteady ship. Far away from all the commotion. Far away from all the action. But it feels as if I am burying my head in the sand. It feels like hiding. And it almost makes me cut more skin off my fingers than I do off the potatoes. Me, a man known for his high stress tolerance, is now turning green and yellow from stress. Because I am not allowed to interfere with our surging fate. I have no influence. No voice, no helm, no supervision, no nothing. Overcooked vegetables, square potatoes and crispy, black sausages is what I have got an hour later. An ungrateful task, which is still gratefully received by the unexperienced hard workers who are trying to keep the ship from sinking.

For too long, I am stuck hovering below deck filled with tension about the rescue. My relief about Ty's presence only too soon makes way for concern about his seemingly passive attitude. He subtly asks me whether everyone has been provided with a decent meal, after which I without saying a word and invite all the non-steering sailors to the table. This means only a few can sit down. We all sit at a small table. Tensions are high. The silence is unbearable. I do not know how to behave and keep filling the plates. But I am just not able to swallow any food. And I cannot answer any of their questions. I have no view on the panic situation. No status, no view, no timeline, no action radius.

The roles are switched after lunch, without an interim group reflection this time, and I try, moving heaven and earth, but I must remain below deck. Ty firmly announced that to me, before he called the MT for the switch on deck. My head is bursting with relevant ideas. About who definitely shouldn't be navigating. Who should definitely not be made captain. But my voice is unheard. And my input remains zero. I am not even allowed to supervise the necessary transfer. Have they really taken a good look at this? Would this turn out for the best... without my guidance?

The afternoon seems to last forever. I try to keep myself busy with what appear to be useless activities. But I am still focused on the uncontrolled rocking of the boat, the aimless changing course of the ship and the ominous noise of the water and the wind. The storm settles as the evening falls and everyone on the boat calms down again. But not me. I cannot wait for our next group reflection. To finally share in the desperate encounters. In the untenable stress situation. The shifting of responsibility. Not having their entrusted helmsman. But the conversation we have later that night, the one I listen to with mixed feelings, does not contain any of this.

There is not much talk about panic and despair, but they do give each other compliments on their calmness and strength. On their overview and decisiveness. As soon as they top that with a compliment on my behalf for the trust given to them, I cannot but show them my good side, by showing them my dark side. Entrust them with the fact that I did want to resolve things for them. Did not want to hand over the helm to someone else. That in fact, I hadn't put my trust in them. Which seemed completely out of order. I have to admit that. I won't easily forget how desperately lost I had felt. Not being able to follow my primary instinct and come to the rescue. My instinct to manage the crisis, run it, solve it, rescue it. Powerlessness is unbearable. You are not allowed to do anything, you are not able to do anything. Out of pure misery I cannot think of anything else but to count. The number of potatoes, the yellowish coloured panels on the ceiling. The dots on the curtains, the stripes on the chair upholstery. The amount of hair standing on end on my left arm. No, powerlessness is killing. Waiting for the storm to blow over. Until finally you can relax and breathe. Do your own thing again. Go on, like you used to do. Like you are used to. Or maybe with a different perspective? With a wealth of new experiences you gained from the storm? With newly gained competences, recently discovered qualities. This most certainly applies to my department managers. But does it apply to me as well?

I won't easily forget how positively surprised I am. Not just with the end result, but even more so with the newly discovered qualities of my competent managers. Peter will always be Peter. He will never change. Even on this ship he talked about the technical aspects of sailing, instead of talking about the team building process. My previous attempts to let go (not more than a few) always resulted in disappointment. Going on a holiday or even going away for just a few days had always had a negative effect on business. I couldn't hand over the helm to others. Wasn't allowed to. It always turned out like that. So why is it possible now? Is it because of the entirely different situation? Do my people just 'happen' to be good at dealing with crisis situations at sea? Or was I the one who had made a change? Handled the situation differently. Just like during my absences from the company, I was now also stuck with my hands tied behind my back, not being able to respond to things that needed attention. Just like during my rare weeks 'off', someone else had taken over the control of the company. But in these cases of me being absent, I had always made sure there was a detailed transfer of information beforehand. And now there had been no question of any transfer at all. No instruction. Moreover, and according to Ty the most important thing, there had been no expectations. The bar was set sky high. By me. The inimitable goal. The expectation nobody would ever be able to meet. I would rather not have had this painful conversation with Ty. But I am just going to have to deal with it, I fear. The painful truth. The only way my people could have done a good job, is by doing it exactly the way I would have done it. And for which there is only one right way to do it, and that is my way. An impossible task for anyone other than myself. Anyone but me.

You cannot sail on yesterday's wind

Here on this boat I did not just let go of my role by not helping to save the boat from sinking. I also let go of my people. I abandoned them to their fate. At least, that is how I feel. That is how I felt during the action itself. And the conflicting emotions I am experiencing now, now I notice that my people are handling things better when I am not guiding them. That they can move mountains when I least expect them to. Because I did not expect them to. I can literally entrust my life to them. I was convinced the boat was headed in the wrong direction. That the helmsman wasn't keeping the boat on course. But I now realise that I am not capable of taking the right decisions when I do not have a clear picture of what is happening. That I'd better not intervene when I am not able to perceive the whole picture. And even if I am aware of the entire picture, sometimes it is best for me not to intervene then either...

If you cannot beat it, go around it.

The next compliment addressed to me is about the welcome meal I had been able to prepare and deliver despite all of the commotion. I decide to interpret that, as "everyone was equally important today, both the captain and the cook." Of course, I can never be sure if they actually mean it since I am their manager, but today I just do not want to think like that.

During a quiet moment, Ann asks Ty and I if we have a minute. Of course we do, so the three of us take a stroll along the deck. We discuss what happened today, but halfway through a sentence, she interrupts me. We stop walking. She hesitates. But wants to share something. She is in doubt, until she just spits it out. It is Peter, she says. He seems absent. Not involved. Does not participate like the rest of us do. He says he has trust, but keeps staring at the ground. Something's not right. This prevents us from becoming and acting as a team.

Ann's worries are clear and recognizable. Ty points out:
'No matter how hard it is, you can always share what is on your heart and mind'. He does however make a clear remark:

> *'The best thing you can do is to talk to someone, not to talk about someone.'*

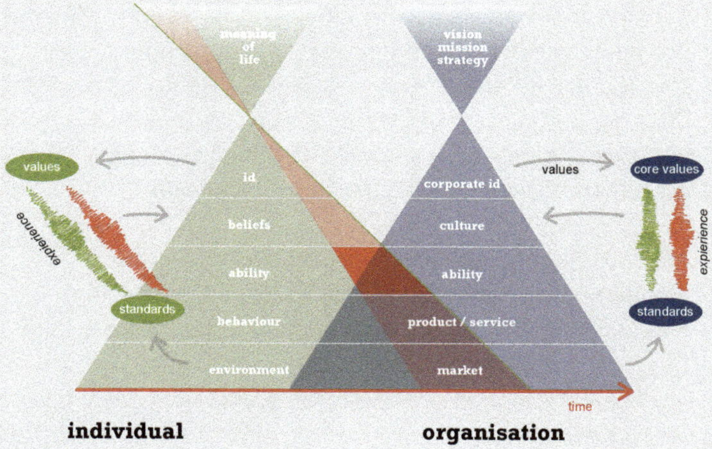

What is happening?

The boat trip offers new insights and extraordinary shared experiences to all MT members. Because of this trip, the management team comes to different conclusions. They discover qualities and competences they hadn't been aware of/weren't using while working at RTech. They are also experiencing that the importance of a role is completely independent of the ranking of this role in a company. While taking a boat trip, they experience the concept of equality, without it being mentioned.

Roy is impressed by the fact that he is complimented for his role as a cook, because he feels it is a subordinate role.

There is room for trust within the MT of RTech, based on these shared experiences. Except for the production manager, who unlike others, is only showing appropriate behaviour. He claims to have trust, but his non-verbal communication shows the opposite. This is noticed by Ty and Roy, as well as MT member Anne.

Reflection

Imagine yourself in another role within your organisation. Instead of sales, you will be production manager, or finance manager. For one week, instead of being a director, you will take on the jobs that are less paid for in your organisation.

What would this teach you that you did not already know?

6 Building the future

A chain is only as strong as its weakest link.
Unknown

The rough weather has kept us from accomplishing our sailing goals. But there is one essential goal that has been established extra strongly by our sailing adventure: a foundation of trust. It feels good to be on steady ground again, and the next day we continue our trip on land. No more journeys on the wild, rough sea. No more journeys through high and inaccessible mountains this time either. We continue our journey to a rustic farmhouse over flat land. We are able to relax and settle down whilst enjoying coffee, tea and some local delicacies. It makes it easier to calm down and not feel pressure knowing that no further roles need to be defined. The roles are clear. Aren't they?

There are red and white chequered curtains, a fuzzy, soft-looking carpet and colourful, lifelike paintings of sheep and cows. What a world of difference. Not just different from our recent wild water adventure, but also different from our familiar working environment. Heavy, dark beams characterise the angled ceiling of this rural meeting location. We all take our seats on red and white chairs, which are standing in the middle of a room around an imaginary table. All MT members are checking the room with questioning eyes, looking for the conference table.

As agreed beforehand, I am not standing in front of them, but I am taking a seat in between my colleagues. Ty is the one standing in front of us this time. And when everyone is seated, he starts talking. Next to him there is a flip-over board with some key words written on it, to give us an impression of today's programme. But the big white paper does not really reveal much. Today's programme is as much a surprise to me as it is to the others. I have not done anything in preparation for this and also do not have any expectations. Especially after the boat trip we took the last few days. This is new to me. And to my people. They do not know me like this. I do not know myself like this. I only know I am doing what Ty wants me to do. It is part of my learning process. Of our learning process. Besides, during our boat trip I hadn't had time to finish the preparations I had started at home. So, I am somewhat forced to enter into this unprepared. But the trust that is emerging, enables me to actually let go just a bit.

'No table?', Ann suggests. All eyes are on me. But I do not have an answer. 'No table', Ty says. 'A table is just an invitation to lean. It enables you to sit back, play with your pencils and partially hide behind a table. But I want you to engage yourselves that is why there is no table.

We are going to spend most part of today setting a goal for RTech for the next years. It is a in our common interest. Therefore it is an important common subject of discussion. Because of the storm outside, we are inside to build a new future. Together we are going to give meaning to a new spot on the horizon. A meaning we fully support.

Then we are going to analyse RTech's current situation using a SWOT-analysis. Knowing where we are now and knowing which direction we want to take, enables us to set course for the future using the right knowledge and tools. This does not mean that the organisational development will turn out exactly how we plan it, Ty says. But it will enable us to keep focussing on the spot on the horizon and adjust our course if needed. We will be doing this together, since we will be taking the company to a new level together. Because we all want to make the most of it. That is our team goal. Not just for today, but for all future group sessions. And most importantly, for the next few years.

'We have already started. Today we are taking this further. We are going to embed RTech's vision, mission and strategy into the present. So, it becomes feasible. We cannot achieve this in one day. You can use next week to process today's results and to experience new things, because you'll be returning to your role with a different perspective on things. Next time, we are going to translate this enrichment into your vision, mission, strategy and core values.'

Begin with the end in mind
and start at the beginning
Stephen Covey

'Where do you want RTech to be in three years' time?', Ty continues. All eyes are on me. But before I start talking, Ty clearly yet compellingly signals me to keep quiet. It remains quiet for a long time. Until one by one, my managers all come up with suggestions. "More customers, generating a stable turnover" Ann suggests. "A financially healthy organisation, that can withstand another storm" Bill says. "Technically perfect products, that sell themselves" is Peter's dream, "bet we have that already" he adds a bit agitated. "To go with Peter, a technically perfect storage room would be nice. Now we really have to work hard to get things done." Richard says.

Hesitantly, but surprisingly insightful. And unanimously, we all 'simply' want to go back to the situation before the crisis. Only slightly better, because of course we do not want to go back, we want to move forward. Grow. Keep growing. No more crisis in our newly set future.

'So you all want to go back to the situation before the crisis. It is just that we cannot turn back time. Which future goal do you want to set?', Ty legitimately asks. Again, all eyes are on me. But this time I am keeping quiet. Curious about other insights, new perspectives. And I must admit, I do not have a straight answer to this question myself. It remains quiet for a moment. Until

Peter, for the first time during our session, takes part in the conversation. Not in response to Ty's question. Not in response to the goal we are setting for RTech. But he merely talks about the purpose of his own presence. And Ty's presence. On all of us being here instead of at the office, where our presence is much needed. 'When can we go back to just doing our jobs?' he asks Ty; Roy doing what he is good at, all of the managers doing what they are good at, including me, and you doing what you are good at.'

'I am lucky to be doing what I am good at right now,' Ty says. 'And what you were doing has brought you where you are now; in quite a stressful situation with RTech. So somewhere along the line something must have gone differently than expected. It is crucial to find out what went wrong together, in order to prevent this from happening again. Are you in Peter?'

Peter starts mumbling and Ty suggest a 10 minute break to have a cup of coffee. During the break, when everyone heads outside, I notice Ty staying behind with Peter. I give Ty a short questioning glance to see if he wants me to stay. He slightly yet clearly shakes his head and then I also leave the room to catch a breath of fresh air together with my colleagues.

> *Surrender to what is.*
> *Let go of what was.*
> *Have faith in what will be.*
> ***Sonia Ricotti***

Once again everybody has taken their seats opposite the flip-over board, which says 'strategic goal' in huge letters. This morning, our goal is to formulate an initial start towards this goal, making it an attractive prospect. To make things less pompous and/or abstract, Ty explains that it involves drawing up a picture for RTech's future together. The constructive brainstorm following his explanation, will result in an initial start towards a new vision for our company. Together with its' partners, RTech develops and produces innovative products and corresponding services, which are an added value to both the company itself and its' customers. This enables us to respond to customer wishes as flexible as possible. We work in a sustainable way and aim for long-term and sustainable customer relations.

This is a nice ending to a productive morning. Ty points out that it is a nice starting point for developing a vision. It is a bit boring now, and it misses the "WOW-factor". It just needs to be fine-tuned, but it is a start. He asks us to take the time to let this vision sink in and think it through, so we can fine-tune it during our next session. Just rethink this vision and add things to it yourself, so we can make positive changes next time.

The strategic goal of course is future-oriented, and we have to play the game with the cards we are holding in todays' reality. After the lunch break we are going to SWOT. Focus on RTech's Strengths, Weaknesses, Opportunities and Threats. To some of the MT members who already know what this means, this raises a smile. They explain this means nothing more than making a list of all the pros and cons. Ty does not argue with that. He points out that we are going to experience a different way of using a SWOT. Indeed, it is about pros and cons. However, more importantly, it is about how you are going to use it afterwards.

Back to the reality of today. We are going to closely examine RTech. Where are the opportunities on the market? What is our competition doing better than us and what other threats are we encountering? What is RTech doing right and what can be improved? These are all questions which discuss a range of different topics and Ty consequently asks us to 'prove' our answers. 'What evidence do you have for this? Can you show me? Can you show me some examples that prove the opposite? These and many more questions lead to many discussions. In a positive way! Because after all, we all share the same goal for

RTech as an organisation. It is not a class room setting at all. We do not just sit, listen and talk, but we actually do something; we actually write, brainstorm and build stuff using elements such as LEGO® blocks to turn off our rational, analytical mind and let our primary vision take the lead. This stimulates our creative thinking and the energy it releases is just great. The post-it notes are literally flying around at times. Fun, enjoyable and most of all, it is efficient.

> *Action without vision is only passing time,*
> *vision without action is merely day dreaming,*
> *but vision with action can change the world.*
> ***Nelson Mandela***

After our snack Ty points out it is time to combine all of our visions. He calls it the confrontation matrix and he explains that, by combining a company's strengths and weaknesses with the opportunities and threats from the environment, we will be able to draw conclusions and set priorities relatively quickly. Since we are all curious as to what is coming, we follow Ty's instructions.

We individually rate the different combinations between our strengths and opportunities within the market. We do the same with our weaknesses and threats. It is quite hard to take so many decisions within such a short period of time. Our brains are working overtime! When we are all done, we hand over our findings to Ty. He puts them all into his laptop and a few minutes later he shows us our own group profile.

To my surprise, this group profile shows many resemblances to my own profile. Could it be that the other MT members share my thoughts?

Ty triggers the release of a remarkable level of energy within the group by asking a few simple questions. 'What are we going to do with your company's strengths, combined with the market's opportunities?' he asks. 'Exploit them' is the answer of Ann and Ty nods approvingly.

'So, what are you going to do with your internal weaknesses, combined with a market opportunity? It would be a shame to miss the opportunity merely because there is a weak spot in your organisation, wouldn't it?' 'Does this mean we have to strengthen our internal organisation, so we can grab the opportunity?' Bill asks. 'That definitely is something you are all going to work on tomorrow,' Ty replies. Ann and Richard are also enthusiastic. But Peter still is quiet. 'What are your thoughts?' Ty asks him. 'If we just make our products technically perfect and ship them to our customers, we do not need the sales department. Customers will come to us and the products will sell themselves. The only thing we have to organise is an interface that collects the orders.' That blunt response seems to be a direct attack on Ann, but she wisely decides not to reply.

Ty points out that everyone within the team has the rights to his or her own beliefs, but we do have to deal with all issues as a team, and this team also consists of a sales department. It is a great idea that everyone is thinking out of the box about the future of RTech, but the thought should have some kind of realistic content. 'The risk is that we will build castles in the air' Ty explains 'How many medium size organisations do you know that do not have a sales department?

'Oh, I am a technician. That is not in my comfort zone and I do not care about that.' Peter replies and for him that says it all.

'How are you to use your strengths against the market's threats?' That is a competitive advantage for us, it is our added value compared to others!', Ann calls out. 'This is what we need to tell our customers, to emphasise the reasons why they should stay with us. Competition!' The atmosphere keeps getting better. Finally it is becoming clear to my managers that they can take matters into their own hands. They are now literally experiencing what it feels like to be in the driver's seat.

'Okay, so finally,' Ty says. 'What are you going to do with your weaknesses, while there are still threats coming from the market?' If we deal with our weaknesses immediately, we might stay ahead of the threats'. 'Your ideas on dealing with the weaknesses quickly is good, yet there is something else you could do as well'. 'I would start cooperating and try to find partners, whose strengths are our weaknesses', I add. And I realise that this means that all this time I have turned a blind eye to strategic partnerships with other companies.

'Now we have got our priorities straight, I think it is time for dinner', Ty says. Time has flown by and now it is already 20.00 hrs! Before we each head to our room to freshen up for dinner, we have got enough material to work with. We will take it with us next week and you are free to add things if needed. For now, let us relax and enjoy the drumsticks, seasonal vegetables and French fries. In my opinion, that sounds better than my square potatoes.

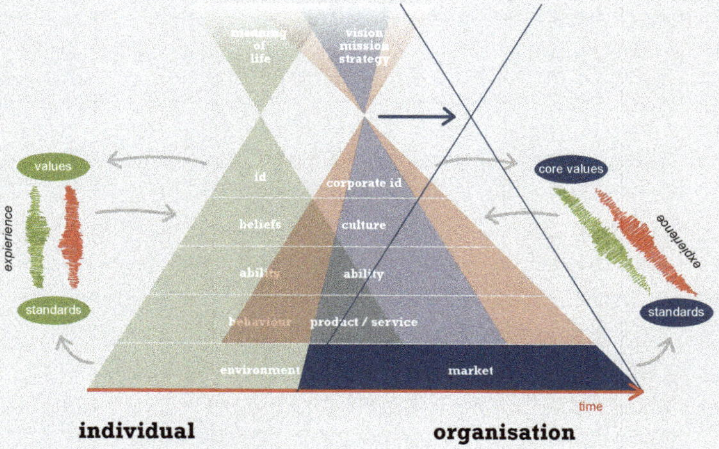

What is happening?

What we see is that we have set a new vision, together with strengths and weaknesses, opportunities and threats in the blue part; RTech as it is now. This way we can keep the good things from the current organisation for future use. All the things that need to be improved can be focussed on the future goal (the vision), so no energy will be lost on needless ancillary matters that add nothing to RTech's desired future.

The most important switch RTech has made now, is that in the past it made assumptions on the quality and strength of its products. Now RTech really wants to listen to its customer and respond with appropriate products and services.

Switching from a product approach to a customer approach is a huge leap in the mindset of employees. This means things need to change within the company culture (blue) and within the personal beliefs of the employees (green).

Reflection

In the previous reflection, you were asked to describe your organisation culture in three to five words. Did these words describe the current or the desired situation?

If they described the current situation, you can ask yourself if this is a culture that represents the standards of your customers. And now a conscientious question. Do you know this for a fact, or do you only think that?

If the words reflect a description of the desired situation, you can ask yourself the question what changes you should make in your culture, to bring the internal organisation in line with the desired culture.

The management team. My MT. While talking things over with Max I finally realise how much expertise there is amongst my team members. I have not noticed this until now. Not just in everyone's own department. But even more so as sparring partners. Ty inviting them to share their thoughts, has made them realise that they can influence the changes in the organisation. In fact, that they are partially responsible for these changes. And all the while they were convinced that they were only responsible for their department. That they needed to do no more than focus on and guide their colleagues, planning, budgeting and managing their part of the organisational process.

Still I get the impression that this extra responsibility is much more a relief than it is a complication of their role. Ty and I are picking up on many enthusiastic responses. Peter only seems to be getting more angular and more blunt in his behaviour. His technical knowledge is important of course, and he was the first employee of RTech. However, now he is the only one just hiding in his box and not cooperating with the others.

At the same time, I am starting to realise that I do not have to figure out everything by myself. That sharing responsibility does not mean you are not taking responsibility. That sharing worries isn't a sign of weakness, but in fact it opens the door to understanding and new possibilities. That an invitation to share thoughts isn't a sign of failing, but something which could lead to surprising results. On the one hand, my MT members have become more motivated and open, because they finally feel heard and appreciated. On the other hand, they are providing enlightening and profound insights into the market.

I have been listening to information which was all completely new to me, all the while speechless and frantically writing everything down. Market opportunities, customers' wishes, threats from new market entrants, developments in the technological area etc. When it comes to strengths and weaknesses in RTech, I am quite surprised by the welcome suggestions. Positive as well as negative of course. Some hurt. Some affect me personally. But to be honest, if all had gone well, we wouldn't be in this situation. And if we cannot be honest to each other, these days off site are useless. So you just have to take it all in. And I do not agree with everything that is being said. But both Max as well as Ty told me that listening is often far more gratifying than talking...

> *When you talk, you are only repeating*
> *what you already know.*
> *But if you listen, you may learn*
> *something new.*
> ***Dalai Lama***

It is the pros that impress me the most, not the cons. And surprisingly, my role as director is much clearer than it was before. Indeed, for the first time in my career as a director I am a participant in such a session. Normally I would be the initiator, now I just give my opinion, like everybody else. Every time a decision is made, Ty asks me to confirm and summarize it. The decision remains a team result, confirmed by someone with the final responsibility. This way we create support for the company's future and everyone takes their own responsibility.

But still I worry. Increasingly, during the days back at the office. We are all working very constructively, but the red figures light up even brighter now I am sitting behind my desk, despite the hope I got from the days off site. We have made many plans, but I cannot wait to take real action. Now. Because we are not there yet. Our problems are far from being solved. I worry about Peter's behaviour. He has to start changing directions, to prevent collision. In my head there are several options, which I do not share.

When Max aptly indicates that problems occur in the past and solutions lie in the future, I gladly let him in on my conclusion: I realise that I can accomplish more by controlling less. Max supports this vision and then asks me what will become my main priority professionally, if controlling things isn't going to be it. I cannot answer right away, but as I am talking, I start getting ideas. Networking; have outside meetings, establishe contacts. And my priority for the company internally will be to guide my people and give them space.

And before he left, of course Max had to give me something to think about over the next few days:

> *'What are the risks of freedom to an employee?'*

7 Rebuilding

'How do you eat an elephant?'

It takes a while before everyone gets the question. It takes a while before silence returns. Everyone is staring at Ty, their mouths wide open and all full of anticipation to hear the inspiring answer to this bizarre question.

'One bite at a time.'

It is obvious. We are on a day off site for the third time now and we are starting off with a joke. Even though Ty continuous his story with a rather serious expression on his face. Before we start running, it would be nice to know which way we are going. We have already set our final destination, the desired goal. But the commotion of the day and the crazy plans we have made, might make us forget to define rules as to how we are going to reach this goal.' This is his way of reminding us of the importance of HOW. So today we are going to focus on formulating our core values. How do we want to cooperate? What is important to us as a group? Only then we will be able to actually connect with the result we have set as our goal.

'If you do not know which way you are going, every direction would be ok. If every direction is ok, everyone will head for a different one. If everyone heads for a different direction, your company will reach a standstill.'

Bare white walls and modern art. Large windows so we can see the beautiful yet grey city skyline from this eighth floor. There is a large table in a corner of the spacious room and there is a circle made out of eight stylish, blue chairs in the centre of the room. A world of difference compared to the farmhouse we were at a week and a half ago, finding the keys to unlock our new future. We won't be inspired by sheep and cows on the wall today. We won't be calmed by the green outdoors on the other side of the windows. But there will be professional calmness. It is professional like you would imagine professional to be, when you read the definition of the word. Calmness coming from the modern architecture. From the impressive view. From all the whites. No unnecessary fuss, no frills. It is calmness like you would imagine it to be from a definition yet to be written. So, we can create our own definition today. In this company of outspoken managers. With all our individual abilities and shared responsibilities. Continuing along the inspiring energy and ideas we got when we were at the rustic farmhouse. Learning from all the experiences we have had in the meantime.

'The role I represent within my department has suddenly become more meaningful, now I feel part of the company as a whole.' 'Sharing thoughts takes me off my island, enabling me to manage specific issues within my team.' As soon as one person takes the first step, other people will jump on the bandwagon. Being truly honest. A selection of our first experiences during the past week. But they are certainly not all positive. 'Production kept going, so I had to keep going. It was just too hectic, so I have not had the time to think about our great plans and ideas'. Time and routine are the bottlenecks most mentioned. 'I am sorry, but I got stuck in my routine straight away and have not even thought about it up until now'. 'We now know we want to do things differently', Ty says, 'it is good to talk about this and about how we are going to deal with this'.

What is positive about this environment is, that it gives everyone the opportunity to talk about his experiences openly. The others listen, without judging. At most, they ask someone for further clarification. It is a relief, this atmosphere we have created. There is no truth. No right or wrong. There is only experience. And plans to make and fine-tune.

In theory there is no difference between theory and practice. In practice there is.
Albert Einstein

But still the ambiance is changing the moment we start elaborating on our experiences. Defeat, the sense of failure. 'I had so many plans, but I just cannot seem to make a start'. 'I want to, but I just cannot. Not right now that is'. 'We were supposed to do things together, I know, but I have not, I am sorry'. The fact that it is a common sense of failure, offers some comfort. The moment I decide to show my vulnerability and share my sense of recognition, it seems to release a great deal of tension among the others.

I had felt like such a failure. I had felt so miserable. In the short term, it feels so good to be unconsciously incompetent. As soon as you become conscious, it hurts really bad. This is at the expense of one's functioning, and then we will be lost. Until you recollect your starting point. Until you realise that in the long term, it will benefit us all. That there are in fact possibilities. That this will make us grow. If you want to. If you put your mind to it. It is going to be hard, but it will be worth it. I cannot imagine how I would have recovered from this without my personal coach. And when. And at what cost. Desolation turns into understanding and respect. And especially into hope.

Ty also adds a great deal of hope. The fact that we talk about our negative experiences means that we are all conscious of them. Our behaviour hasn't changed, but it did feel different. Because in our minds we are already taking giant steps. Our ability is growing, but the changes we have to make in our behaviour cannot keep up the pace. This inevitably causes frustration, but that is just the way it is. It takes time to change our behaviour so that it matches our ability. And it starts by being conscious. And that hits us hard. Feelings of failure and disability are part of the deal unfortunately. It helps to know you are on the right track. That consciousness is a good start. Instead of running around like chickens with their heads cut off and acting without thinking and then hoping for the best, we start off with a common plan. Working towards a common goal.

'You have already been working on that by focussing on a number of RTech's weaknesses and starting up an improvement project. So, as an organisation, you have already set things in motion. And when things are in motion, you just have to persevere. The same goes for a car accelerating from standstill costs the most fuel. Congratulations. You have taken off on your journey towards the new RTech. Which brings us back to the HOW. How is this awareness going to help us move forward? How are we going to continue this journey together and how do we make sure everyone is pursuing the same course? How are we going to make sure that our goal remains a common goal?

'Okay, I think the situation can be defined as follows. You all have a general view of RTech's future. And you have all been working very hard to improve some of your internal weaknesses. In short, you have all been doing really well. But you are still not satisfied and there is still a sense of agitation and impatience. Today we are going to use those feelings to add focus to the plan.'

While Ty is talking, I realise he is right. We have a general vision about the future of RTech, but because of our lack of focus, it seems like everything is happening at the same time. And when everything happens at the same time, you do not finish a single thing and everything comes to a standstill. At that moment, I feel my own impatience and the urge to do it all by myself again. When I set priorities, at least we can move on! Make RTech profitable again.

Ty hits the brakes. During a ten minute break, he tells me that it is wiser to prioritise as a team, not top down. That smart working is not the same as hard working and in my case, it means that I need to shift from thinking I am the only capable guy, to learning that others can be capable of creating the same or maybe even better. I need to move from old beliefs to new beliefs. That is what I was going through a few months ago and now my people are going through this. It is quite a painful step in the process of gaining the desired unconscious ability.

After the short break, Ty decides to explain what we will be doing the coming period. 'If I want to run a marathon and I find out that I am capable, this certainly does not make me happy. Because at that moment I am aware of the fact that I am not able to do it. When I use a training programme I can improve my ability. This is a conscious process. Only when I have made a habit out of running the marathon, I am no longer aware that I am capable of running one. The same goes for companies. You have to practice in order to become better, to create endurance and gain power that lasts.

But there is a difference. In a marathon, the rules are clear. You all start at the same time, you run the track and the one who gets to the finish line first is the one who wins. As a company, you are going to have to define your own rules for the game. Each and every one of them is unique. So, every company has its own starting point, is heading towards its own future and is using its own selection of tools.

As soon as we have finished formulating a strategic goal based on our vison, we will set up the rules we are going to have to stick to. Following these rules will give us the confidence that we will be able to realise our vision and our strategic goal. However, we also have to determine when someone will be disqualified, because he or she did not play by our rules

In organisational development terms, it means that we will transfer vision, mission and strategy into strategic goals, which can be measured or observed. Halfway through that marathon we will be able to predict whether we will get there in time, whether we should accelerate or whether we should slow down. The core values will be verbalised, so we can observe whether someone is playing the game by our rules, or whether they are cheating.

Vision, mission and strategy, together with the core values is called "the social compass."
The social compass, together with the strategic goals, enables us to focus on the game and the result.

Ty continues: 'Today we are really going to work on adding focus. Setting measurable goals. Have you thought about the vision we have formulated during our last day off site? We are proud of our renewed vision: *together with its partners, RTech develops and produces innovative products and corresponding services, which are an added value to both the company itself and its customers. This enables us to respond to customer needs and desires with as much flexibility as possible. We work in a sustainable way and aim for long-term and sustainable customer relations.*

Beautiful. This covers all elements. All aspects of our services and customer services. Without adjustments and additions, this will be our first step to accomplishing our final goal. We now have to directly translate these visions into the strategic goal we want to reach within medium term.

Last time we formulated this goal as follows: within 5 years we will be just as big as we were before the crisis, but this time there'll be full support from within the company and we will be more future proof. Now, hardly two weeks later, we still support this for 100%. Still the goal isn't quite SMART. Not specific, measurable, acceptable, realistic and time framed.

That is something we do need if we want to be able to calculate, monitor, measure and fine-tune the steps we need to take towards this goal. What we thought was very clear and 'unambiguous', sounded fuzzy, unspecific and filled with open doors to Ty. And that generates useful discussion. Even though our group 'only' consists of five people, this results in five different perspectives. The funny thing is that, although our intentions often correspond, we appear to disagree because we all use different words to explain ourselves. Having an objective third party present, who's not responding from a content point of view, is a necessity. Even though Ty has been with us for months now, he still has an independent vision on content while guiding the process. Today I notice yet again how constructive this is.

Even during the preparations, because it allows me to get a clearer picture of what to expect. Ty told us that in every company, there are both optimistic as well as pessimistic goal setters. It is remarkable that this becomes so incredibly clear during our session today. Ann turns every opportunity into profit and uses these thoughts to set goals that are almost unrealistic. Bill on the other hand, sets his goals extremely low. Like you would expect a man with a financial background to do, I think. Financial people are often less positive, Ty told me yesterday, because many things can happen before it all works out below the line. We have also talked specifically about Peter. A technician in heart and soul. He keeps pushing towards the technical perfection of his products. It is annoying me and I can see that others are annoyed too. Ty asked me about my expectations or even my hopes for him. If we are going to set goals, he needs to stick to them. But for now, Ty does not see Peter showing any will to change. Even worse. Peter is getting blunter by the week. It is a possibility that he will come around and start changing when he knows his targets. Unfortunately, at this moment Ty observes more resistance than he does progress. I admit that I also have doubts about Peter's behaviour, but his technical knowledge is very important to RTech.

We also talked about our goals, that will be translated into very clear plans, by which we need to navigate. Integral, cross departmental, I am responsible for reviewing the agreements we made and to address my management team, if they do not stick to the plans. And at in the same time I have to avoid the pitfall of doing so myself.

Ty said that he expects me to have to correct Peter multiple times before he will start changing. He advised me to organise a few meetings with the individual members of my team, to set the expectations for the future. In time, that will make it easier to review whether the expectations are matched and the agreements are met.

Yet Ty did inhibit my way of thinking. 'What would you do if you were aware of the fact that your job depended on certain goals which you were entitled to co-formulate?' 'But', he adds, 'do not let yourself be influenced by your expectations. Think about them and then let go. Enter into the session open-mindedly, listen without (pre)judgement and act upon the things you actually hear, see and experience.'

Having no expectations at all is almost impossible to do. Fortunately, my hopes are bigger than my expectations, therefore I am still capable of giving Peter the benefit of the doubt. He asks many questions: 'Why this percentage? Why do we need to measure that as well? Can't we just go ahead and do it? We cannot measure everything?' etcetera. Legitimate. For the large part. At one point, I get slightly frustrated and irritated, and at the same time I notice the other MT members share this feeling. It seems like he does not want to measure anything at all. As if Peter is consequently sabotaging us from setting measurable goals. This is obviously expressed by his non-verbal communication. He has a negative facial expression, never agrees, is constantly looking at the ground and is purely focussed on the internal organisation.
Ty remains calm and objective, enabling us to continue no

matter what. That enables us to keep moving forward. I do not know how he remains so patient, but it is probably normal for him. He uses a method that views the organisation from four different perspectives.

From a financial perspective, you always look at the past. Regarding the internal processes, you look at the present and whether this can be improved. Regarding customers you also look at the present, but now with an external focus. And regarding sustainability you obviously look at the future as well.

Like I said before, it takes intense discussions to set the SMART goals. After spending an entire day including half of the evening working, the result, which is one piece of paper containing nine goals, feels like an unsatisfying result. Still, it has been a crucial initial step to start monitoring things. Because you won't know what to change in the organisation, if you do not first decide what you are going to measure.

Financial perspective

- a gross margin of 35% on products and 65% on services within 3 years' time.
- a solvency of more than 30% within 5 years' time.

Customer perspective

- Customer satisfaction will be at least 8 (on a scale of 0-10) within 3 years' time. We scored 6.3 in our latest measurement two years ago.
- Customer exit is nil.

Internal processes perspective

- Failing costs will amount to less than 1% of the revenue.
- Employee satisfaction will be at least 8 (on a scale of 0-10).
- Absenteeism will be less than 2% annually, measured by calculating the total number of hours lost to absenteeism in a year as a percentage of the total number of available working hours.

Sustainability perspective

- 80% of product innovations will be designed for customers we know are going to buy the product.
- Ongoing search for a more sustainable and environmentally friendly production process, that reduces waste and fossil energy usage by 25% and obtain ISO environmental certification within 3 years.

Ty reminds us of the fact that we have now determined our finish line. But we have not set the rules of the game yet. We know when to score, but we have not decided at what time someone is given a yellow or red card yet. Or when someone is given a compliment. With this in mind we say good bye to each other. It is so unreal how time just seems to be flying by. Incredible what we have accomplished today. Not just on paper. I am really curious about the experiences we will be gaining during the coming weeks. Experiences the people around us will be gaining after we show up at the company and practice a new way of responding and acting, based on the insights we have gained over the last couple of weeks. But Peter still worries me. It appears he really does not want to change.

One week later, while I am sitting at the table with Max, he asks me if I really thought it was such a good session. Because he is picking up on some aggravation and irritation, he says. Max thinks my story sounds far less cheerful than the meaning of each of its individual words. When I try to deny this, try to point out once again what the physical result of the session is, I feel the anger building up inside of me. I feel my jaws contracting and deep wrinkles appearing on my forehead. He is right. I am pissed. I am done with it. Things have got to change and I am going to call Ty to let him know I want to end Peter's contract.

I have been waiting far too long, hoping things would get better. Hoping his behaviour would change. That he would start cooperating. But it is not going to happen. I am done being patient. Peter is going to have to come round very soon, because his future at RTech is at stake. Maybe even RTech's own future…

Not long after that, I am talking to Ty, who actually gets my point but specifically asks me not to fire Peter right now. 'What if you would ask him again why he puts up this much resistance? Does the new RTech fit Peter?', Ty asks. 'You have to keep in mind that it is also a learning process', Ty says. 'Right now, we are learning from Peter as well, from his specific knowledge on production. We do not know why he is putting up resistance. Perhaps, he feels that he is taking the lead. Feels like he is doing everything he can, but cannot seem to move forward because the company does not want to go forward. Because the company does not understand him. He is experiencing it just like we do, the pulling, but we think he is pulling at the wrong end. Subsequently, we think he is putting up resistance. Things are getting more and more clear to me; I am going to have to set up a meeting with Peter. What is Peter's personal intention? What is his motivation? Honestly, I have not got the faintest idea. It is something I am going to have to ask him. Then Ty asks me: 'Is he unable to go along or is he resistant to head in the same direction as the company? What does it take for him to go along with RTech? Does it provide more opportunities for both Peter and RTech than the costs involved?' I have to leave all these questions unanswered. And more and more I wonder whether Peter still fits in RTech. Ty immediately responds: 'Does the new RTech fit Peter?'

It is a fact that up until now, Peter has always been an added value to the company, but he is now showing undesirable behaviour as far as RTech goes. Is he aware of that? Is he prepared to (co) operate? There is only one way to find out. And again, I'll only find out by talking with Peter, not about Peter. As the tension is building up on both sides, it is crucial not to postpone this any longer.

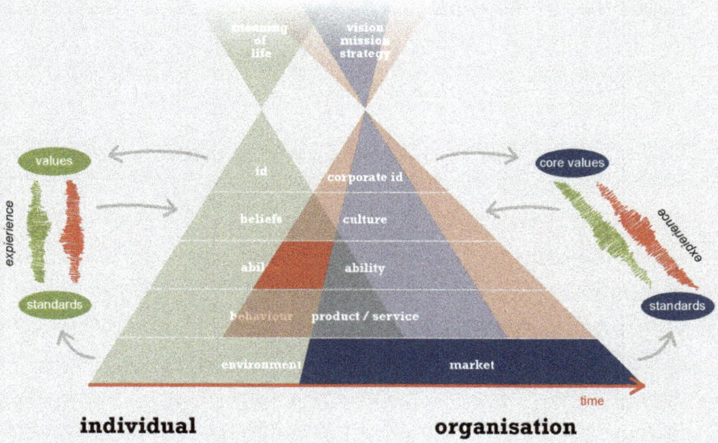

What is happening?

Earlier on, the model showed us that we are not just welcoming a new market, new products and services, new capital and a renewed culture and company identity. But we are also saying good bye to a part of the market, to part of the products and services, part of the capital, the culture and identity. In terms of complexity and ease you cannot separate welcoming from saying good bye. Is it easier to integrate a new product into the company process than it is to get rid of an old one? Is it easier to hire a new colleague than to fire an 'old' one?

Is Peter really positioned in the red part of this picture? That part is about Peter's abilities and therefore shows whether he can still be considered to be an asset to RTech. Or is he one level higher. Where personal beliefs might collide with RTech's new culture. From Roy's perspective, he is on the verge of deciding to get rid of an employee. The side of saying good bye, of letting go. Because this employee is unable to or does not want to head in the same direction as the company. Is the company growing too fast or is the employee just not keeping up? Or is the company taking a right turn, whilst the employee can only (or maybe only wants to) take a left turn? They do not fit together anymore. This could only be temporary, if the employee starts moving in the same direction and subsequently starts fitting in again. But if it is permanent, if this employee refuses to head in the same direction as the organisation, then it will be best for both parties to say good bye.

Reorganisation is like getting a new job without having asked for one. When a watch manufacturer decides to start building wall clocks, some employees will have no problem adapting. Not necessarily effortlessly, but training, motivation and other necessary support can make the process run smoothly. But there will always be employees who keep focussing on the ergonomics of the wrist. The ones who keep applying former knowledge to the clocks they are building now. They will not benefit from a working relationship with a wall clock specialist. Even more so, you won't be doing them a favour by keeping them in this (new) job that no longer is a good fit for them. Although it does not generally feel you are doing them a favour.

Reflection

Take a look at your own situation. There are thousands of reasons for not doing certain things, while knowing that you are in fact expected to do them. The things you are able to do, but postpone because you do not feel like doing them right now. If you are not able to do a certain job, but you want to do it, then it is something you can learn to do. If you are in fact able to do a certain job, but you just do not feel like doing it, then it just won't happen.

Motivation is more important than ability. But both motivation and ability are necessary to get a positive result. If you are able to do something, but you do not want to do it and your environment accepts that, you will not do it in the future either. Often without consequences and sometimes with big consequences. I talked to entrepreneurs who finally found out that they had been making a loss after 18 months, because they had neglected to keep the accounts.

Think about your own activities, the ones you postpone. What risk do you take if you postpone them?

It felt good to be back at the office. The focus we have gained by setting new goals brings an entirely different dynamic to the work floor. Still it turns out that being away from the office for one day, has resulted into me having to put out fires now I am back. That is something I do not want to be doing anymore. Peter asks questions about additional work in a production run. Bill asks me which invoices should be paid first. When I walk through my building, the cleaner asks me whether the stain on the floor still needs to be cleaned, because he has a knee problem and he has trouble sitting on his knees. I realise that all these should not be my responsibility. I really want to change that pattern. If everyone could take responsibility for his own role, RTech would become stronger, more future proof.

These days off site have been great for our bonding process, for our optimism, for our solution-oriented mindset. If you are involved and future-oriented in such a constructive way, it fills you with hope and energy. And trust in each other as well as in our company. While I am enjoying the improved culture that is taking shape within the organisation, I make the following note for myself to share in our next day off-site: Within the new RTech, I want there to be a culture in which everyone feels equally responsible and is free from crisis situations such as these. I realise that such a culture requires me to replace my being in control to me setting boundaries. Not telling everyone what to do, but showing them the limits to the freedom they have to act upon.

> *'If it is your role to set boundaries, make sure you are aware of your own boundaries. Let us check out these boundaries together, shall we?'*

During my conversation with Max, I do not answer his question. I am still in the middle of telling him my story about our latest MT-day. We do have to set the rules we have to play by. We have already defined our finish line. Next step are the rules. Ty is absolutely right; it is the HOW that matters. Someone might achieve his results, but if they can only be achieved by harming an issue that is crucial to others, then the result you have achieved is merely sub-optimal. Cooperation, working atmosphere, what is important to us as a company? Is this what Ty meant by HOW?

When I talk about this with Max, he fully supports my vision. It is good to overthink the core values', Max says, 'they have to fit both yourself as well as RTech. Not that you are your company, but if you do not fully support the core values of your company, you won't be able to function.' This reminds me of the conversation I had with Peter earlier this week. And I have even more specific questions I wish to ask him. But most of all, I want to give him the space to show me his vision. On Rtech as a company. The role he plays. The growth we have envisioned, the direction we have chosen, the common goal we have set. We need rules, limits within which we are entitled to operate. I am curious of Peter's willingness to operate within these limits. Where are his boundaries? And is he going to respect and abide by Rtech's limits? It will take some getting used to. Peter sees me as a controller. Not as someone who sets boundaries. But I am going to try on my new suit. I am going to take on this new role. I am going to start setting boundaries and at the same time creating free space within the boundaries.

> *'Shall we start by finding out your own limits and formulating your own personal core values?'*

I find out more and more about what is making and keeping me tick during a special, personal conversation with Max. All the things that are important to me, crucial to me, essential to me. On a personal level, this turns me into a person who's becoming more and more conscious. On a professional level, it enables me to become a better leader with obvious skills.

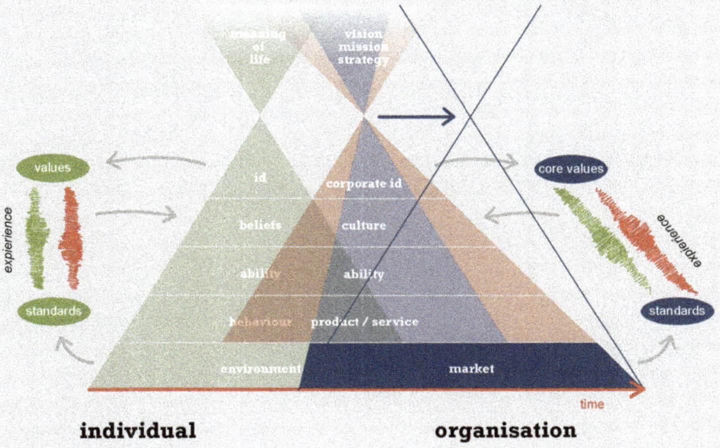

What is happening?

We want to release the tension between the market's changing standard (expectations) and the organisation's current core values. We do this by creating new core values that have to meet two requirements:

1 The core values have to represent RTech. They represent RTech and management has to be able to commit to them, since the core values contain the individual's standard within the organisation. And since being a manager means you have an exemplary role, it is crucial that you are able to commit to these core values. So, you can actually live by these core values and promote the recognition of these values in the company.

2 The core values must meet the market's expectations. It would be best to just ask the market what its main expectations are. Talk to your customer!

Reflection

To what extent have the core values of your organisation been adequately fulfilled? Are you personally prepared to connect with these core values? Do you want to walk the talk based on these core values? Are the core values at the same time in line with the expectations of the market? Its standards? Are you sure? How do you know?

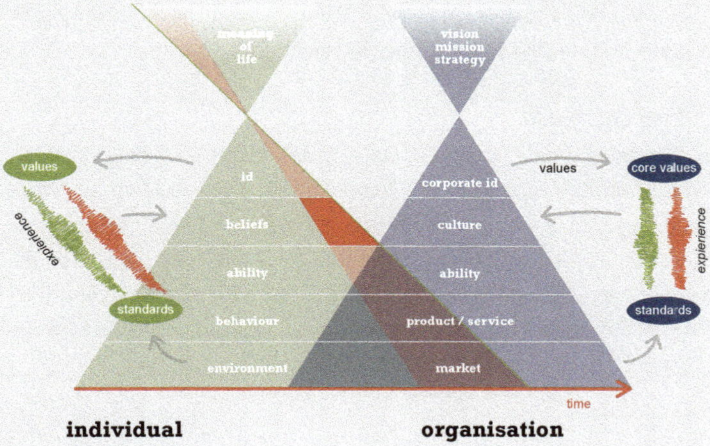

What is happening?

At the same time this means that Roy is going to start setting boundaries and taking control instead of controlling every detail. This is a change made on the level of Roy's individual beliefs (green). Roy used to be convinced that he had to manage his people. They came up with questions, he just gave them the answers.

Roy decided, his people followed. Moving towards the new RTech, leads to a shift in Roy's beliefs. His environment (in this case his employees) changed, causing Roy to gain mainly positive experiences. He relieves the tension between the values from Roy's current identity and the standard of Roy's changing environment by adjusting his belief. The trust he now feels his environment deserves, requires Roy to change his way of thinking. His team seems to benefit from having limits, in which they are free to operate, rather than from receiving instructions.

As soon as Roy has sorted out his new beliefs, he notices he also has the ability to change his behaviour. After which he in fact does expose behaviour focussed on setting boundaries. These changes do not just happen overnight. As soon as you realise you'd rather go to work by bike than by car, it only takes time to get used to your new behaviour.

Reflection

Do you answer questions, you actually think the other person should have come up with himself? What experience are you giving him at that moment? Will he develop into a self-aware person, or are you going to let him have this fixed mindset, in which he does not have to think for himself? What is a bigger gift? Giving all the answers or giving him the gift of self-awareness?

When we look outside, we see the skyline slowly forming a silhouette against the sunlight breaking through. The dull view is getting some colour, the grey buildings are starting to shine. It is a breath-taking panorama, that contributes to the inspiration we need to expand our own views. The atmosphere is good. The setting is rewarding. The temperature is rising because the sunlight is becoming more intense, or because of all the energy that is flowing. Or maybe both. It feels good to make plans for the future together. Ty exploits this by giving us challenging assignments and asking profound questions. Whether we are prepared to think about the question how we would like to cooperate in three years' time. How we are going to make sure we are successful by that time? Because that is what we want. Which culture suits RTech 2.0 as well as the market as we know it now? Of course, the goal is to create a goal in which the current crisis would never occur.

Ty starts again, 'So our goal is to formulate core values that not only fit RTech but also respond to the market's expectations. The core values need deepening, because they are a container concept. Each core value should have its own RTech definition. Every definition is a belief in itself and is detailed in abilities or competences. The competences should be described in terms of behaviour that can be observed. Only then, when we have formulated all desired and undesired behaviour, we will know the rules of our own RTech game. Only then we will have given colour to the social compass. Colour to our vision, mission, strategy and core values. Only then we will be able to make decisions that fully comply with our compass. And the result of these decisions, the result of the social compass, can be monitored through our strategic goals.'

With renewed courage and armed with a pencil and some paper, we get to work. And it turns out to be more difficult than expected. Determining core values isn't easy. Our individual wishes, do not necessarily benefit the company. Our mission is to keep questioning: is it a core value for the company or is it your personal value? And another thing Ty told us in advance: things could get rough. Ann is all for stability and security, but is that a core value of the company? In my opinion, RTech should be flexible. Fortunately, Ty helps us out just when we are about to get rid of this core value. Core values of an organisation and personal core values could either weaken one another or strengthen one another. In Ann's case, does stability mean she does not want the organisation to change? Or does it enable RTech to become a more stable source of income, because it is more flexible? Ann lights up after hearing Ty's words. It is the latter she is referring to, of course. Peter on the other hand, keeps provoking and showing resistance. He translates all solutions proposed by us into mumbled problems.

Ty suggests that we now have to look at the organisational core values, and that we as a management team have to put ourselves in the serving role for the organisation. Putting personal values before the organisational values means that we mix up our personal identity with the identity of RTech. That will blur our vision and will have a negative result on the sustainability of RTech. Let us just look at RTech as another identity. It would be great if, in the end, we could come to the conclusion that RTech is a great tool for fulfilling our personal values.

Peter by the way, keeps challenging us. Not in a constructive manner, but in a continuously condescending, almost sabotaging kind of way. 'Customer-oriented? The numbers below the line are what really count, from an accounting perspective.' 'Flexibility is a weakness. It is a sign of having no backbone'. I decide to leave the room with Peter and talk to him privately about his negative attitude. He points out that he does not have any confidence in the future and isn't at ease with the way we are handling things. 'You do not even take responsibility yourself, so why should we have to take it? You have put us in this position and now we have to find a way out for you?!' No matter what I say, the heated discussion does not stop.

The accusations hit me hard, although I do understand them partially. The best thing for me to do now, is to ask Peter to behave a bit more positively. And to have a conversation with someone who might help him see that the way he is behaving at the moment, is neither positive for himself nor for the group. And let him know that I cannot tolerate his behaviour any longer, that he is removing himself from the team like this.

It is not until later on, when I am talking to Ty about the day off site and in particular about my encounter with Peter, that I realise that this has been going on for days, weeks, months now. But what is most clear to me now, is what is happening during the days off site. Peter is the only one constantly sabotaging the process of making things measurable. 'The more measurable the results are, the more insight we gain in everyone's responsibilities.

> *'If you are not going to take responsibility, how measurable are you going to formulate the results?'*

In the evening during diner, you notice how everyone is still enjoying today's results. Each of the MT members is still excited about our latest creation. At least that is how it feels. Even the waiter has to join in on it when he is taking our order. Ann is wondering how innovative the menu actually is. Richard wonders about the flexibility of the kitchen with regards to Bill's list of 'forbidden foods'. RTech's new core values seem to have been fixated in our minds.

We have defined the 5 most important ones: customer orientation, not just for the benefit of the customer, but even more so in cooperation with our customers. Performance orientation is next. Meaning there should be an added value for both parties, for the customer as well as for ourselves. Number three is innovation. Unanimously chosen and selected, because to high-technology companies such as our own, it is extremely important to deliver innovative products and services. Furthermore, we want to be flexible in handling customers' desires. The last one is responsibility; we use sustainable methods to cooperate with sustainable relations.

During diner, everyone is being appraised based on RTech's new core value laconically yet seriously. I am very interested to see how things will evolve next week, when we will be measuring the entire company both consciously and unconsciously. But up until now it seems to be more logical and familiar, than it is new and drastic. Even Peter seems to be getting along with it quietly, although everyone is speechless when during desert, Ty suddenly asks Bill 'Just how COPORIF (customer orientated, performance orientated, responsible, innovative, flexible) are you?' We are having the best time right here and now, but will it stick with us? And the core values are completely clear to everyone in the MT. This is now our shared dictionary. Now all we have to do is act upon it.

We have written down RTech's new core values. I am going to put them up against the wall tomorrow and I cannot wait to hear the responses from all the other employees. They are all informed on the WHAT. Now I slowly want them to learn about the HOW. They'll be getting more and more involved in the development process towards RTech 2.0 and the HOW in the coming period. Hopefully, terms such as customer orientation, performance orientation, innovation, flexibility and responsibility do not just appear out of thin air.

Hopefully this will mostly lead to recognition and acknowledgement. Possibly it will lead to questions, which we will only be too happy to answer. With our renewed vision in mind. Because there is a direct link between the core values and the vision. We produce innovative products and corresponding services, which are an added value to both the company itself and its customers. We respond to customer needs and desires as flexible as possible and we not only value working in a sustainable way, but we also value sustainable customer relations.

I look back on this vision process with great satisfaction while I am driving home after this successful day off site. We have accomplished so much. We have not only observed and formulated, we have also set out an approach for all the loose elements. We do not just have clear goals and values, but we are also busy paving the ways to take us there.

The only thing lacking is a clear action plan, a helicopter view on everything we have decided. What is our first priority, and what is not? Will we tell our customers now, or later?

Ty suggest that the last option is probably the best. The moment that employees understand what is expected and get familiar with the social compass, they will play the game by the new rules. The social compass and the strategic goals are the guidelines for each decision. He asks me to define the projects that RTech will adopt.

'We only take on projects that are customer oriented and innovative, that have added value (result), that can be organised with flexibility and that add to RTech's responsibility towards the market.' While I am memorising this, I do not just feel proud, I also feel the tension ebb away in my shoulders, as it reassures me and offers me hope and confidence.. We have accomplished an amazing result within a relatively short period of time. For now, they are just plans.. However, solid plans. Now we have to follow up on them. And we are only at the beginning of this.

When Ty and I are preparing the next step, it turns out that we can combine several of our plans. Actively involving our employees in improving the internal processes can be combined with giving them the responsibility to adequately implement the social compass. A participative approach, Ty calls it. To get employees more involved, thus creating support for the core values and making sure they are communicated within the organisation. It is an effective and motivating way to let the employees immediately know what is expected of them. We even want to let them take part in their own assessment system. A performance management process will be the next logical step we should take in the coming months.

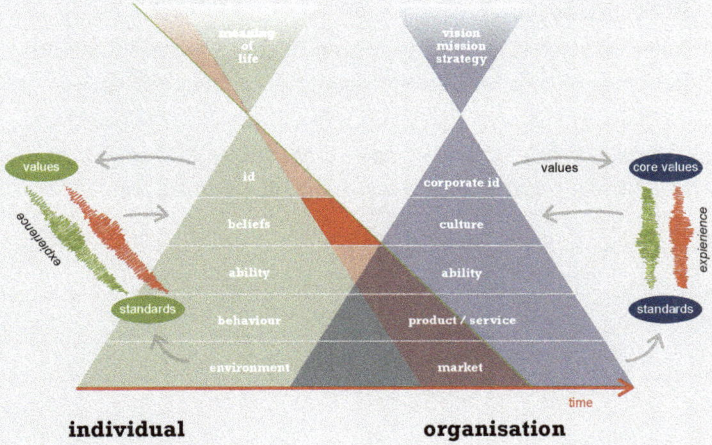

What is happening?

As soon as the future vision and strategic goals have been formulated and the core values have been defined, the renewed expectations on the employees' behaviour no longer match the old situation. Employees will have to adjust to the new COP-ORIF -culture. This might cause them to be confronted with their own personal beliefs.

By working with the employees in a participative way, they will experience confidence. This will enable them to connect with RTech's future. This will strengthen the motivation as well as the will to improve both the organisation and RTech's situation.

The employees have a say in RTech's future, within the boundaries of their responsibilities. The MT has set these boundaries at their level. Employees will be able to implement the boundaries at their own level. They will be gaining positive and negative experiences. Both the positive and the negative experiences will help RTech to further implement the tasks in order to achieve the strategic goal.

Reflection

Imagine yourself asking your employees to seriously rethink their roles and activities, giving just a few boundaries. How would they respond? Will they make it easier for themselves or are they ambitious and make it harder for themselves. You should just try it! You will be in for a surprise! Guaranteed!

8 Performance Management

I frequently pass on Max's questions word-for-word to Ty. This is a remarkable situation, having two different coaches who influence and affect me on two entirely different levels. Max does not focus on RTech, he only focuses on me. And he expects me to come up with all the answers and solutions, while I often want him to do so. Ty focuses on RTech and the people that work within the company. Or at least, on the MT. Ty asks many questions as well, but this coaching relationship is based on the coach providing us with the necessary tools to answer the different questions. Existing tools used by others which have already proven to be effective. But also models and tools developed by himself, which have also proven to be effective. Still, the answers and solutions are given by the MT and Ty, like Max, is the catalyst, who helps me/us to uncover the solutions. Somehow, they are pushing us into different directions. Provoke us to get us moving forward faster. And we are moving in a positive flow by reflecting and fine-tuning exactly at the right time. It is great to see how much energy and motivation this has given the MT. It is cool to see how I am so much better at handling my pitfalls now. But how do I get the rest of the company to go along? When I walk the halls I hear the mixed feelings people are having about the changes in the company. But what do I actually know about the employees' experiences with the new RTech? The renewed culture, the new core values which are suddenly very important, the company's changing navigation system. They have to go along.

'Is that so? Does everybody have to go along?'

I look at Ty in shock. Haven't enough people been fired? I have already halved my staff, so I take it that the rest can keep their jobs?

'Even when they are unable or unwilling to go along with the company's growth?'

I have to process this information, let it sink in. I realise that he has struck a nerve. I feel the deep wrinkle in my forehead I got from having to fire people over the past year. Emotionally, that experience has cost me ten years of my life and I want to make sure I'll never have to do that again. I want to support my people, guide them personally if I have to. I have carefully selected my employees and partially because of that, I have some very valuable people working here. I am not going to fire them just like that.

> *'Even when they are unable or unwilling to go along with the company's growth?'*

Ty is repeating himself. It is one of his bad habits, I notice. Clearly, I have to address this question. My priority is running this company. When an employee does not fit in the company (anymore), then I must put the company's interest first and let him or her go. But not without careful consideration, I quickly add. Of course, I am thinking about Peter. That discussion isn't over yet. We will soon find out what the best solution is for both parties. Just like before, I hope he'll get his act together and perform the job he is familiar with in the company as he always has done. But exactly how familiar is his function within the new company compared to the function he used to have within the old company?

The next question Ty asks me, is exactly the same question I asked him a few minutes earlier. How do I know what is actually going on within the company? How the employees are actually experiencing the new company? I only know what the MT tells me and the things I hear in the corridors.

> *'Is this your interpretation of the experiences, the interpretation of your MT members, or are these the actual experiences of your employees?*

I have to confess that it is all just hearsay. And during the MT meeting two days later, the MT members are telling me the exact same story. 'What do you see happening?', Ty constantly asks. And 'How can you be sure that this is correct?' Asking, asking, asking, is the only thing we can do to come up with a better analysis. Otherwise, it will be nothing more than our own, often subjective, interpretation. During the MT meeting, we agree to go out and actually connect with our employees. How we do this, is totally up to us. We will share our positive and negative experiences at this table in two weeks' time. Together with Ty I decide to literally take the plunge and go out onto the work floor again. It has been way too long. I have been up in my 'ivory tower' for far too long, only to come out when I had to go to a customer. Customer contact is now more and more Ann's job, so I can focus more on the internal issues. To the work floor it is.

There is a lot of commotion in most departments, because they are not used to me looking around. Yet, when my intentions become clear, many of them respond in a more positive way. Unfortunately, I cannot do much more than observe all the current processes. The pressure is high and the employees do not have much time to start a conversation with me. Until I visit Bill's department. There is an apparent quietness, because all of the employees are concentrated. There is a lot of typing going on. The radio is switched off, while before it was always playing, wasn't it? I thought I heard that radio when I was passing that room.

I watch Alex. 28 years old and one of the accounting employees. He is so busy and concentrated that he does not even notice me. After a short period, he notices my presence with a bit of a shock. I ask him why the radio is off.

He watches me and says that the pressure is so high, the radio became more of a nuisance than a source of pleasure. I want to sit down next to him for a small talk about work pressure.

'Please do not' Alec says. 'I really do not have time for that right now. It you want to talk to me, we can do that during lunch. This is my first priority now. Shall we have lunch together in the restaurant? Then we can take the time to talk to each other.'

No more than two hours later we are having a sandwich in the tastefully decorated company restaurant. Everyone around us is looking surprised, because nobody can remember the last time I have eaten lunch there. The people he normally has lunch with walk past our table, even though there are four available seats left. It looks like a serious talk. And in fact, it is. Only the setting is friendly and relaxed.

This is the first of many valuable peer lunch meetings. Not all of them are as informative, but they all give me good insight into the internal experiences throughout the different departments. I sometimes share the table with one colleague, and sometimes I sit with five at a time. Me showing up in the company restaurant and employees starting conversations with me, is becoming more and more 'natural' to everyone. As it is to Dirk.

It turns out that Dirk has quite a lot he wants to talk about. According to him, things have been done the same way in the production department for years now. Work pressure is high, too little insight in customer needs and desires, hardly any personal input. The second item is what scares me most. Not only has the department been on a standstill regarding the new RTech, but more importantly, what does he mean by little insight in customer needs and desires? You work at the production department, it is all about customer needs! Dirk is going on and on. I am astounded by his story. By all the ins and outs. By all the examples he is giving. The frustration he shares with his colleagues. The attempts they have made to talk about things. Losing not just motivation, but also some of their valuable colleagues who, in the end, had decided to take on another job elsewhere. By now the restaurant is empty and getting cleaned, but we continue our conversation undisturbedly. 'My colleagues and I have no clue what the customer wants,' Dirk says, 'we only know what Peter wants us to produce.

Leaders become great,
not because of their power,
but because of their ability
to empower others
John Maxwell

Coincidence, if it even exists, makes Ann come up with the same signal that week. Customers talk about products not complying with their wishes. Ann's vulnerable attitude appears to enable customers to open up and discuss this with her. I focus on what Ann is saying, without thinking too much about my inability to notice that our customers feel this way. Customers never seem to get exactly what they had asked for. They always seem to get something slightly different. Sometimes even more than they'd asked for, but never exactly what they'd asked for. Customers are relieved to add that extra work is never added to their invoice, but that does not mean they are satisfied. Even before I am able to ask Ann to check this with Finance, she mentions that she has already talked to Bill about this. And that he is just as surprised as we are. There is an MT meeting tomorrow, and I suggest that we are going to search for the cause together. And, more importantly, for a solution.

The employees from the other departments are more positive. Some say they have to get used to the changes. Others did not even seem to think of it as 'change'. They all indicate that everyone is more involved. They feel as if their manager pays more attention to them. Or in a different way. Or both. More attention is being paid to the relationship instead of just to the result. While I am listening to these responses I realise that this is exactly the change we had to make. Without me being aware of the fact that this was exactly what was missing. What RTech was missing. Changing from spreadsheet management to relation management. Without losing our focus on result. Suddenly I recall the start of this painful yet informative road to recovery. The moment I read Ty's column. The moment I realised I had to pick up the phone and call him. Because in fact it is all about the how. How are my employees going to achieve results? This is RTech's new culture. Our new and joint set of beliefs. In a new order: people first, result second. When result is lagging behind, there is no use in working harder. There is no use in stretching the results even further. To push people even harder. The only thing you can do is tackle the cause of the problem and find a sustainable long-term solution. That is the way it works and I am aware of it. It is clear that my managers have gained new confidence; when they use behaviour-based management, result will follow only naturally.

> *If you can't handle pulling it push.*
> ***Berthold Gunster | Flip-thinking'***

It is not just the managers who have to get used to things. Many employees also still have to get used to the new RTech. Many people are still trying to find their way in translating the new core values into practice. What is expected of me? What kind of behaviour complies with that expectation? it is often quite difficult for the management to make clear what they expect from their employees. That is logical, since they have to gain experience first. It takes time. I am aware that they are out of their comfort zone, but I am confident that things will turn out for the best. Yet I am going to check this with Ty, see what he thinks, based on his experience with other companies that have had to deal with this as well.

> *'A company won't change unless the people change. And when people change, the company changes.'*

At first this sounded cryptical, but it actually makes sense. I understand what he is saying right away. Is that another cultural change, I wonder. The thing we initiated when we were on the boat? Ty nods and adds: 'The most underestimated and sometimes underrated company capital, is its human capital. Even now, machines and technology form such a large and important part in our everyday lives, yet undoubtedly the importance of people is only increasing. Automation is still spreading, but still there is nothing that can fully replace the work done by people. Replacing human contact by avatars and online forums for example, will never match the added value of personal contact. Especially with regards to motivation and listening. Even though listening is often easier for a machine than it is for a person. Even though machines keep getting better at interpreting words. The underlying emotion, the underlying limiting belief, the importance of one's personal situation, will never be comprehended by technology. And to be honest, some people will never comprehend it either. Therefore, we have created lists of special competences that can be used in application and assessment procedures. Whether these competences are being implemented or not, will be noticeable on the work floor and visible from employees' experiences. There'll be a big difference in conduct when you compare a department led by a people manager to a department led by a manager who is focussed on figures.'

'How do you want to achieve this within RTech?
How do your MT members lead their departments?'

Within RTech I see Ann is really good with people. I notice this by the atmosphere and productivity in her department. And judging from the results she is achieving with her customers. She really knows how to get the full facts from the customer. I am less enthusiastic about Peter's competences. There is agitation and distrust throughout his department. This has an immediate reflection at the end of the line; the (financial) results. No matter how you look at it, this department is not doing well. I have already talked to Peter, but according to Peter, he is not the problem. The problem is cross-departmental, according to him. I fully support the idea of finding solutions to deal with unsatisfied customers throughout the entire organisation. But my gut feeling says there is no use in filling gaps anymore. We have to deal with the real cause right now. Ty laughs. Apologizes for laughing because, after all, it is a serious problem. But he adds that he is also enjoying my point of view. Because it reminds him of how I approached the same kind of issue a year ago. 'Bury my head in the sand?' I ask him. But he means the development I have gone through from being a solo-trouble-shooter to being a director who shares responsibilities. From merely being responsible and acting, to facilitating the search for causes and to possible solutions. From clinging on to gently letting go. Towards the new long-term approach that has replaced our attitude of filling gaps. Towards a sustainable, objective people-oriented way of leadership. A sense of pride. Well earned, if I may say so myself. I have worked really hard on that. But speaking of work, back to this moment, preparing for tomorrow.

> *'When you start the meeting tomorrow, what will be the preferred solution and what will be your plan B?'*

In my mind, I have already thought about how I want to solve things. An old habit. But I know better by now. A solution is not a solution unless it is supported by the MT. So, I aim to find a solution in cooperation with my MT. I do not want to impose a solution on them as a director. I hope Peter will see what is going to happen if we keep doing what we have always done. I hope Peter will understand the importance of our new core values, of the new RTech, of our new and cooperative way of working. I hope Peter will understand and, as a consequence, will act accordingly.

> *'How are you going to make sure that you will make a decision, even if there is no solution? So, if Peter does not act accordingly, what will you do?'*

Then he no longer fits his role at RTech.

> *If you do not decide,*
> *the decision will be made for you.*

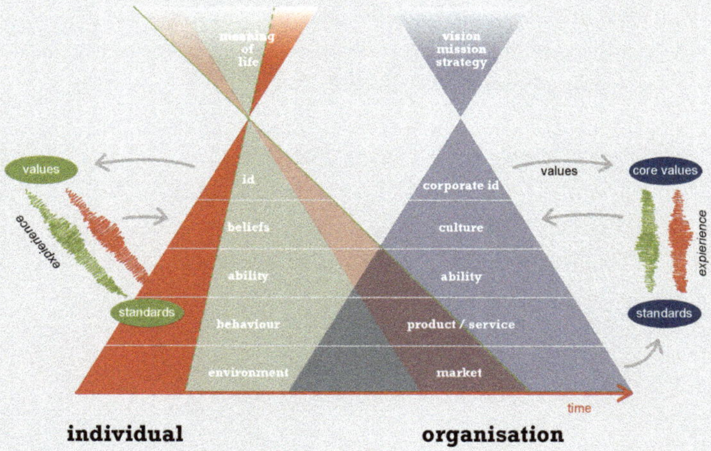

What is happening?

During a process of change, you often see that not everyone is able or willing to go along with the process. Peter sets a striking example. In the model, you see that the individual Peter still does not overlap with the organisation as much as he should. Since Peter's beliefs are so contrary to the organisational culture, he is not capable (ability) to adjust to the new situation. He only shows a little of the conduct desired by RTech and in practice this has turned out to be insufficient. On the right side of the green pyramid Peter does not show the desired behaviour. At the same time, he does show behaviour that is no longer desired within the renewed organisation. This is shown in the left side of the green pyramid.

Looking at this from Peter's angle as an individual, the following will happen. Should he be part of the development, then Pete will experience tension between RTech's standards and his personal values. The most important question is, whether Peter wants to change. The next question is, whether he is capable of changing.

Based on the conversations with Peter and the remarks he made, Roy comes to the conclusion that Peter isn't willing to change in compliance with the company's direction. That is why Roy is considering whether it would be ethically justified to let this person keep his role. Keeping someone shouldn't just be beneficial to the organisation. It should also be beneficial to the person himself.

Reflection

Leadership is an art as well as a profession. And meanwhile we see a lot of organisations in which the best employee on a certain subject is promoted to a supervisor's role. When we make the best carpenter a supervisor, we risk losing a great carpenter and creating a bad supervisor. Especially when a supervisor is not educated in leadership skills, the organisation is taking a huge risk.

Take a critical look at your organisation and at yourself. How many of your managers and supervisors have earned their role because of their management skills? Or did they just get promoted because they were good at a certain subject and you assumed that therefore they could be a manager as well?

The specialists in your organisation are worth their weight in gold! Be proud of them and cherish their knowledge and experience. But be careful in promoting them to a manager's role without training their management skills. Because not every specialist makes a good leader or manager.

What could you do in order to improve knowledge and experience on one side and at the same time improve your organisation's leadership skills on the other side?

My gut feeling is clear on this. Peter's leadership is the problem and it has got to change. 'Would that solve everything?', Ty asks. Yes. No. I do not know. And I cannot and won't rely on my instinct; it has to be justifiable. Towards the rest of my company as well as towards myself. And I also want to have better insight into the results of the cultural change within our company. Is that possible? How can I objectify RTech's situation? I ask Ty whether he has some kind of tool to measure that, if possible. It does not even take him a second to answer my question. Ty proudly tells me about a measuring method he has developed himself and which has been certified by TNO. He calls it a cultural monitor. Several times a year, you use it to ask your employees about the current situation with regards to the core values and any other issues. They can also indicate their wishes concerning each of the questions. Between each measuring point, there is a possible gap. After mapping all the gaps, you can bridge these gaps by asking the employees to actively work together on a specific gap. By assigning employees to different project teams to diminish a gap, you constructively work on organisational development. These projects give employees the responsibility to work on the desired culture. They also learn that they all can influence the future of the organisation. This usually has a positive effect on motivation and, as a consequence, on the productivity and the success of their own project. By asking the same questions several times a year, making the same analysis, the size of the different gaps will show the changes that occur throughout the year. This measuring method enables us to focus on actions and result, ensuring the best chance of success. This sounds like an incredibly insightful model! Why didn't he tell me about this right from the start?!?

'What would have happened if I had suggested this right from the start? First putting out the fire, then mopping, then building. What do you know now, that you did not know then?'

Touché! It would only have caused more stress. And the effect wouldn't be as significant. I would probably have focussed on result even more, instead of on relations. Not on behaviour. I would never have given the MT and the employees their own responsibilities. 'Would there have been any room for this cultural change?' No.

There is a heated discussion going on at the conference table, after Ann has shared her issue. All alarms go off when customers are unsatisfied. The problem appears to be obvious: customers are not getting what they have asked for. How are we going to solve this? 'Improve project control,' Ann proposes. How do we control our projects? Bill wants to respond, but Peter interrupts. 'This does not involve a project, but a product, that is what the customer wants.' Bill clearly states that all the extra work has to be stated on the invoice. Heads are nodding at the table. All but Peter's. That does not surprise me at all, because that is exactly the point where customer needs and desires seem to estrange from production and invoicing. 'If only the product is technically perfect', Peter says. 'And what if that is not what the customer wants?', I ask him. 'If the customer wishes to settle with an eight instead of a 10?'
'Then he has the wrong supplier.'

At times like these I could use some of Max' insightful words. This dilemma is really bothering me. Part of me knows, the other part does not want to know. Saying good bye to Peter isn't easy for me. Budget cuts are insignificant. This resignation is solely based on the way Peter functions within the company. Max nods: 'As the director of RTech you see the importance of the company, but for you as a person, your emotions are important as well. That is ok. It is actually quite logical. It is not as if you do not like Peter as a person. On the contrary. But the behaviour he shows as the manager of RTech's Production department does not benefit the company.' Yes, exactly. And to that I must respond as a director, because that is my role. Max nods. 'What if you let him stay at RTech? Are you confident that his behaviour will change for the benefit of the company?' No, the last couple of months have made that very clear to me. He has been given every opportunity. He has received sufficient feedback, but hasn't acted upon it sufficiently. As a director, I know what I have to do, so why is it so difficult? 'You are dealing with two personal beliefs,' Max points out. It is now up to you to prioritise them. What is more important to you: Peter liking you or your company becoming healthy? Both choices have different consequences. Which consequence are you willing to take?

The strength of the team is
each individual member
The strength of each member
is the team
Unknown

The second bilateral conversation I have with Peter is difficult for me. But I know there is nothing else I can do. I am going to be straight to the point, because that is best for him as well. I start the conversation by saying that I cannot imagine him being happy the way things are going. To me, a customer-oriented organisation like RTech isn't beneficial to a person like you. To be honest, I think it would be far better for you to be in a production-oriented organisation. Peter does not say anything, but his expression tells me that he hesitantly agrees with me. As of now, I am going to relieve you from your duties, and we are going to work on a solution together. Peter's eyes are suddenly wide open. The following minutes are filled with unfinished sentences consisting mainly of words like 'how' and 'why'. In which he keeps pointing out the added value he has been to RTech all those years and what he still has to offer.

When Peter's finished, I ask him to sit down again. You know what is expected of you, being the manager of your department, I tell him. You know the social compass and you know what is meant by COPORIF, RTech's new core values. Subsequently, you do not implement these core values. You say 'no' to everything. RTech has taken a new direction this year. One that, as we have all noticed during our days off site, is more compliant with our customers' wishes. It is expected of all RTech's employees, including myself, that we head in that same direction. But if you do not go along, it means that RTech is no longer the company that benefits you most. It is not making you happy. You are not making us happy either, though this might sound a bit harsh. It would be best for you to go home and let it all sink in. Let us schedule a phone call next week to set a date so we can continue this conversation calmly.

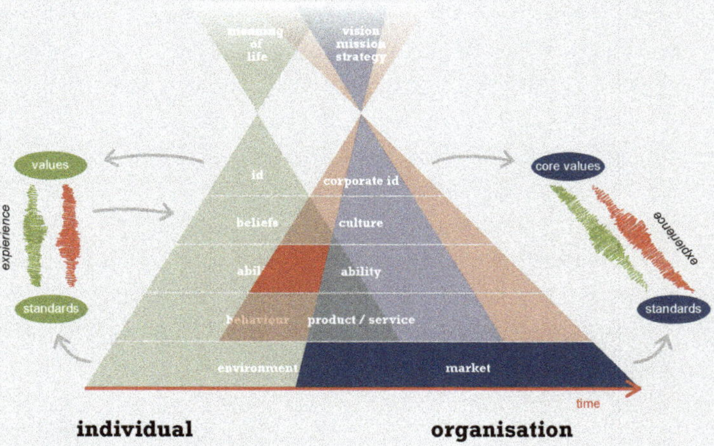

What is happening?

Peter's literally stopping RTech from changing. His 'not going along with the changes' does not just influence his own functioning and well-being. It also stops the necessary developments within his department from happening. Which in turn has a negative effect on the areas in which Peter's department gets in touch with the customer and/or with other departments in the company.

In the model this is shown by the red field in ability and the tension on the far-right side; Peter not willing and/or being able to go along (ability) results in RTech not being able to completely release the tension between the standard of its customers and RTech's own values. Between the customer's expectation and the company's culture. Peter not changing subsequently leads to his entire department not being able to change, which undermines the company's future sustainability.

Roy's decision to let Peter go, will enable the company to comply with her customers' world of experience (standards). His resignation does not mean that the organisation will immediately be able to accomplish all the changes. It does however eliminate an obstacle in her process of change.

Reflection

How many of your employees are present because of the personal relation you have with them, instead of their functional role? How would this effect your organisation?

9 Pushing through

Peter's resignation comes as both a shock and a relief to the MT. To most of them it does not come as a surprise, which subsequently comes as no surprise to me. Immediately after my conversation with Peter, I have called for a meeting with all the MT members, so I can announce and explain Peter's resignation. This way I can answer their questions and talk to them about the proceedings. Ty adds another item to the agenda, namely the current and desired way of dealing with this news by the MT and other employees. The request to answer this question openly and honestly, is granted without any issue. Showing our vulnerability within the MT has been fully accepted, assimilated and has turned out to be very helpful. When Ty mentions that all our ways of dealing with this have been okay, he has taken away all the final barriers.

Some of the MT members have had a private conversation with Peter. Have warned him that he was putting his job on the line. Others thought he was becoming more and more a disruptor, but did not do anything about it. They were 'just' waiting for Roy to take action, they shamefully admit. And at the same time, they wondered what they might or should have done. This question remains unanswered, because we are not all here to judge each other. And we cannot turn back time to do things differently. We are here today to look back and to find a way to move forward. Ty takes out a marker and walks towards the flip-over board. 'We can conclude that there are different ways of handling the situation concerning Peter's behaviour and resignation,' he says. 'Waiting for Roy to take a decision is what we refer to as old behaviour in a change process. The behaviour you were used to in the old RTech. That is okay, as long as we know that we now expect different behaviour from each other and from ourselves. The ones who did take action, have shown leadership. Have taken responsibility.

Like we have set out in our core values. That is the exemplary role we are talking about. The one I am going to keep reminding you of until you have all mastered the role.'

One by one he writes down numerous actions we wish the MT would take with regards to what we were just talking about. Both the envisioning as well as the repeating and the saying out loud of this desired behaviour adds to the diminishing of the step we need to take to actually do it, almost making it feel natural to us.

> *Leadership is practiced no so much*
> *with words*
> *as in attitude and in actions*
> ***Harold S Geneen***

Ann's mind is still filled with worry. Even though she is proud and satisfied that she is now able to recognise the desired behaviour. But what to do with Peter's department? Who's going to be in charge of Production? They cannot remain adrift forever. Is it going to be Paul? Can he combine his work on the work floor with leadership? Or drop this for the benefit of what to him would be a new management role? Would that benefit the department as a whole? Or maybe place an ad, which might be more effective. What kind of manager are we looking for? And are we looking for the same competences we might be expecting of a department manager in a year's time? This also concerns Bill, because we have only recently been able to keep the organisation financially afloat. Not much more room there. So, production cannot be at a standstill, but this department won't be operating as desired all by itself. Something has to be done in order to get things back on track.

After having taken numerous options into consideration, we all agree that we are going to have to find an interim department manager for production on very short notice. An intermediate is easier to find and someone from outside the company brings along a different dynamic. It wouldn't harm to put someone in charge of Peter's department who offers a different perspective on our current way of working. And this person might even be an added value to the MT. Also, appointing someone new means everyone else can keep their own role within the company. This way, role blurring isn't an issue. If you are forced to fulfil two roles at the same time, you are only half fulfilling both roles instead of completely fulfilling them. If you completely fulfil one role, you would score an 8 on a scale from one to ten. If you are only able to spend half your time on each role, then you'll score insufficiently on both roles.

Reconsidering the various different ways of dealing with the situation regarding Peter, Ty asks us to look at it from our employees' point of view. How are they dealing with this? Moreover, how do we want them to deal with this? Because we have to be role models. Because if we do not serve as an example and show them the desired behaviour, how can we expect them to show it?

Ty stresses the importance of the exemplary role very frequently. And by now the entire MT has endorsed this. Because it is very clear to everyone that a good example is more often keenly followed. And at the same time, the reverse is also true. Peter's employees show absolutely no change for the benefit of the cultural change. While all the other departments have shown progression. Things could always be better of course, but the movement is headed in the right direction and it is clearly visible.

It comes as no surprise that the new flip-over sheet remains empty. Not because we do not have anything to say. Not because we do not have a clear view on the behaviour we want our employees to show. On the contrary. Everything we are saying is written down on our own sheet in a similar form. I think we have now come to the point where it is no longer necessary to explain the word exemplary behaviour. We just have to act upon it.

Rumours are increasing by the hour. Of course, Peter's resignation hasn't gone unnoticed. We have to come up with a plan, before panic is going to spread through his department and subsequently all the other departments. Come up with a communication strategy to inform the production department and others within the company. And of course, a communication strategy for the replacement of Peter. 'How are we going to deal with all the rumours?' Ty asks. And what are we going to communicate to our employees regarding Peter's resignation, so we radiate unity?'

In no time the flip-over board is filled with suggestions which are shared by all of us. When all ideas have been written down, we can start duplicating and prioritising. This way we can formulate a clear message that is supported by all of us: RTech has gone through a major change the past year. Peter couldn't agree with the new direction the organisation is taking. This compromised his functioning. We have chosen this new direction to make sure that the organisation is future proof. Therefore, it is of the utmost importance that we all head in the same direction in RTech. Of course, we wish Peter every success in his future career within a company that fits his personal core values.'

The department managers will immediately communicate this message to their employees. Roy will personally communicate it to the production department. We are also sending out an email, so everyone can read it again and to let them know who to turn to with their questions and worries whenever they feel the need to do so. Some people might recognize Peter's behaviour and realise its similar to their own. Who might not feel comfortable in this renewed organisation either. Who wonder whether they might be happier working elsewhere. A few of those employees might have a less legitimate reason to fear for their job, but they are genuinely afraid that this might happen. It is our job as an MT to signal these worries and offer them a platform to discuss these. That is our responsibility. And the more we take responsibility, the more all RTech employees will take theirs. The more we create a culture that is open and honest, the more colleagues will experience and expand this culture. A win-win situation, that is how it feels now and later on this feeling will grow. I feel like a guru doing a pep talk, but I notice from the responses I get from my audience, that my message is well received. It is motivating and inspiring and that is exactly what I want to accomplish. What I want to express. What I want to teach them so they can multiply it. That is my exemplary role. We will be having another day off site in a few weeks, to translate our new core values into perceptible behaviour. That might sound simple and unnecessary now, but Ty assures me that it will be an intensive day well spent. In the meantime, we are going to take care of the communication regarding Peter's resignation, I am going to look for a replacement and we are all going to exhibit our exemplary role more and more. 'For the sake of being complete,' Roy concludes:

> *'Always take your responsibility to share both the successes as well as the difficulties with each other.'*

I keep thinking of the cultural monitor Ty was talking about. It is an appropriate follow-up on all the lunches I have had with many of the employees. It is become somewhat of a tradition that I want to keep up, albeit less frequently. I cannot wait to find out what insights I'll be getting from this cultural monitor. Of course, it is always a snapshot. That is why we are going to schedule it cyclically. I have already gained so much insight from all the conversations I have had. But do they really open up to me? I was positively surprised by the frankness I had experienced during the lunches, but in the end I am still their employer. And of course, I have not spoken to all of them.
On the contrary, I have only spoken to the people who were willing to speak to me. Who wanted to tell their story. Who weren't afraid to ask questions. Who weren't afraid to express themselves.

What if we would ask the entire company the same questions and we would pour the answers into the cultural monitor? What kind of perception would roll out regarding RTech's current and desired situation within the framework of the core values? What kind of perception would we get from each of the departments individually? I have noticed that Finance for instance has a great sense of responsibility, but they point out that they feel unheard at times. And Ann's department experiences such a great deal of freedom, that her employees are now in need of extra frameworks. Within Peter's department, it is exactly the other way around. Since he has left I have only become more aware of the consequences of not going along with the changes of the new RTech. The consequences of old RTech behaviour. These are all examples of the tiny and sometimes bigger experiences gained by my employees and myself within the organisation. We should be able to optimise these by monitoring them. I am feeling restless, yet energetic. Let us just say a healthy dose of impatience. The fact that the change has already led to so much positive motions, is a welcome confirmation. It is eye-opening. And I am not just talking about mine.

They are still used to handing over responsibility to the manager, especially since they are only at the beginning of the cultural change. Thankfully a manager ad interim is in sight, but he won't be available as of today or tomorrow. So the longer it takes before he can actually start working, the more things I have to keep up and running and the more chance there is of all things falling apart. Exemplary behaviour alone won't suffice, I notice, and together with Ty I schedule a seminar for the Production department, so they can prepare for the change that they too are going to have to make. Production itself cannot stop running, so we are splitting up both the department and the seminar day. This way, everyone can start 'experiencing' the change for half a day.

Taking in the culture, as Ty likes to call it. Not just having to listen to an interesting presentation for hours on end. Just a short intro and then experiencing how two of the best actors re-enact the situation so powerfully, that it requires no explanation. Afterwards there'll mainly be silence, followed by questions during the next few days. Courage will grow. Requests to do things on their own will be made more and more. To operate more freely. To get in touch with Finance about the extra work that they are expecting. To take responsibility themselves.

The department is already showing more movement by the time the interim manager Cynthia shows up a few days later. Everyone is still trying to find their way in this new modus. But the atmosphere is opening up and after my conversations with Cynthia I am fully confident that she will be able to lead this movement into the right direction. That she'll be able to motivate and inspire the employees. And more importantly, that she can give them confidence.

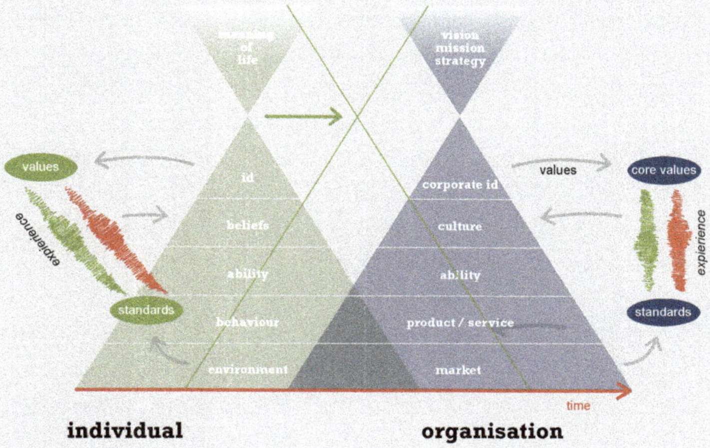

What is happening?

At this moment tension is visible in the model between the individual's standard (caused by his environment) and the individual's values (caused by his identity). For the employees of RTech this means that in the future other behaviour is expected of them.

This tension is influenced by the experiences the individual gains, which have a direct impact on this person's beliefs. If someone tries very hard to meet the new standards and experiments in adapting new behaviour, he leaves his comfort zone and is therefore very vulnerable. When he experiences negative feedback, he will rethink this new behaviour and return to his old behaviour.

Negative experiences will cause the tension to continue or increase, because the distance between the values and the standard remain the same or might even become bigger. Positive experiences will cause the beliefs to adjust to the environment's standard. It turns out that it is safe to change behaviour. As a leader, we have to be aware of this phenomenon. Positive feedback will bring the employee in a growing mindset. Negative feedback will bring him into a fixed mindset. By giving positive feedback, the employee will make a shift to the right, causing a release of tension between the values and the standards. A good balance will be achieved. More tranquillity, making the individual feel more at home within his environment. As an organisation, you do not have a choice: you must inform your employees of the reorganisation and ask them to change their behaviour. And you give them the appropriate learning experiences.

People learn new behaviour by copying it from others and also learn through experiences. Therefore, it is key to provide the appropriate learning experiences to successfully implement changes in the organisation. But giving someone the appropriate learning experience is one the hardest things to do. It requires sharp observational skills and a thorough understanding and experience in the use of conversation techniques to postpone your judgement on a situation and the behaviour of someone else. You must postpone your judgement until you know the intentions behind the behaviour, because if you give your employee a negative learning experience while his intentions were positive, you did not create an appropriate learning experience. The employee will stop experimenting with new behaviour and create a fixed mindset.

But when you succeed in giving appropriate learning experiences, you can stimulate positive behaviour (and experimenting is positive behaviour) and address the undesired behaviour. I call that giving development-oriented feedback.

The development-oriented feedback method

Development-oriented feedback is created by the Z-model of Change®. The goal is still to realize a change in the behaviour of the employee. But this method is more clear in pointing out the desired changes and, as help is clearly offered to the employee, making it possible for him or her to develop. That is why this method is much more effective.

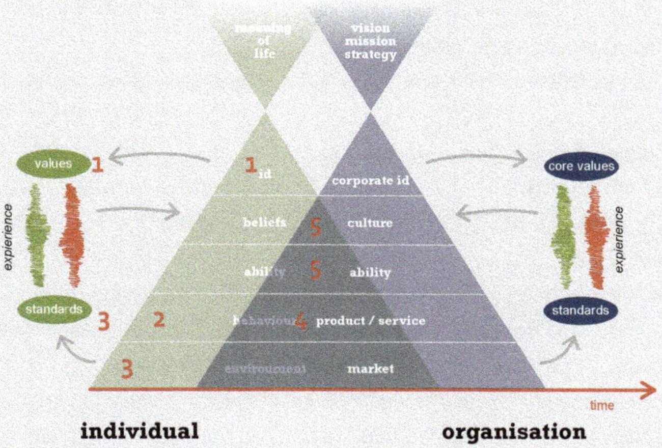

The method can be explained as follows:

1 A compliment on identity level
2 Addressing one's behaviour
3 Link the values stated by the organisation to the negative effect of the behaviour.
4 Formulating the change you wish to see
5 Pointing out the obstacles (beliefs or undeveloped skills) undermining the employees' ability to implement the required behaviour.

For Example

1 You have an enormous passion. You work hard and get a lot of work done.
2 Unfortunately, this has a negative effect on your accuracy.
3 You make a lot of mistakes, while you know how important accuracy is to us. This means I cannot hand over more important work to you, which leads to an increasing work load for other employees and a halt in your personal development in the organisation.
4 I would like you to make fewer mistakes while doing the same amount of work you are doing now, so you can continue to grow and develop and will eventually be able to handle the more important tasks. Because I think you most certainly have the skills and the abilities to do that kind

of work. That would not only benefit you but it would also benefit the organisation.

5 Let us find out why you make those mistakes. How can we make sure you will make fewer mistakes in future? What obstacles are you running into?

The effect of development-oriented feedback

This feedback should result in a conversation between the manager and the employee about the underlying causes of the mistakes. The real cause of the mistakes will emerge. The causes could be work pressure, phone calls, getting interrupted by colleagues or just carelessness etc.
By providing the employee with development-oriented feedback, he or she will at least feel heard, seen and acknowledged. While the manager and the employee can address the actual cause together, the employee will be given the opportunity to develop and to reach a higher level in the organisation. This will initiate movement in his or her beliefs, the employee will be changing out of free will. Because the intrinsic motivation, the self-desire to perform an action or behaviour, is added to the mix when people learn to understand why they display undesired behaviour. The experiences I have had, while creating the 9+ organisations, using this method are extremely positive!

Of course, not all of RTech's current employees will be able to stay. They won't all be moving in the right direction, this has already become clear to us. Only the ones who feel at home in this new environment will be able to adapt to the changing environment. Some employees will benefit from a different environment, some will find a better cultural-fit elsewhere. So letting them go, is also a win-win situation.

Reflection

How often do you evaluate the behaviour of your employees? And do you only respond to negative behaviour or do you also give compliments.
And when you respond to negative behaviour, is that a merely a short response to a situation at hand or do you enter into an elaborate conversation when the behaviour occurs on a daily basis.
And your response to positive behaviour? How would you describe that?

How do you know for sure that the experiences you give others are appropriate learning experiences for their specific situation?

Just as I am switching off my phone and want to head off to the company restaurant, Bill walks into my office and shuts the door. Wants to know if I have a minute to spare. We decide to get some fresh air and leave the building. While we are chatting about this and that, we go past a place where they serve delicious local treats. The lunchroom looks nice and cosy and we find a table in a quiet corner where we enjoy a tasteful sandwich and continue our conversation. He points out that he notices little change in his people's behaviour. There haven't been any substantial changes; accounting is still accounting. So he has lost track. He wants to know how he is going to make sure that his people go along with the change. 'I know I have to give them experiences, but I feel stuck..' I understand Bill's frustration. It reminds me of my own frustrations before I finally got the picture. I decide to let Bill in on part of my story. Hopefully this will make him see that his department has in fact made some big steps already. That we are on the right track. Whatever track that might be. And how we are going to keep ourselves and our employees motivated to continue using COPORIF not only internally within RTech, but also externally.

It makes him feel good, me telling him my story, he says. It gives him the confidence that he is on the right track, despite the questions and doubts that he has.

'Maybe it is a good idea to discuss this during the next meeting with Ty', I propose, and Bill indicates that he will take it into consideration.

> *You must be the change you wish to see in the world*
> ***Mahatma Gandhi***

Ty starts of this brainstorm session by only saying; 'Exemplary behaviour'. This time we are in a former monastery, which has been a party- and conference centre for a few years now. It also serves as a location where retreats are held. To start off a meeting with a mind-altering experience or to end an intense seminar with a relaxing one. Or as a full day escape from everyday pressures. Every now and then we hear soft Asian-like sounds. Like a gong or something that reminds you of sushi and Japanese martial arts. Another world is blending in with ours, while we take our seats at an imaginary conference table once again.

'How do I truly live by the core values of my organisation while playing my role in the organisation?' Ty looks at us inquiringly. Apart from a few Asian-like sounds, it is completely quiet, so Ty repeats the question: 'How do I truly live by the core values of my organisation while playing my role in the organisation? Translating the core values into visible and perceivable behaviour is extremely important. That is what we are going to talk about today. One of the steps we are subsequently going to have to take, is a step we are going to be using in a different way as well. I am talking about creating our own feedback, to make the blind spots within the organisation visible.

Think of your exemplary role as a gift you share with others. Feedback is the gift you receive. It keeps everyone focussed. Let us begin.'

She is only been with us for a week and Cynthia is already joining us on our day off site for a strategic session. Funnily enough it feels good to everyone and this day goes by as if it were just the regular MT members attending. And for now, this actually is regular. The instant click between all of us is quite remarkable. 'We are translating RTech's core values into perceivable behaviour for two reasons,' Ty explains. 'Culture cannot be measured. Behaviour can, as far as it can be perceived. We cannot really judge behaviour, unless we can define the behaviour we wish to see within RTech. Only then a manager will be able to make adjustments in his employees' development and subsequently the development of the department.

The second reason is, that the defined behaviour can be judged by your employees. We will use the cultural monitor to ask all employees to judge the behaviour we are defining today in the current situation as well as in the future desired situation. The difference between the current and the desired appreciation is called a gap. Employees will start up projects by themselves, to diminish these gaps. This way they will have an active role in creating the desired COPORIF- culture in RTech. We will give them the responsibility to start showing COPORIF behaviour themselves, thus spreading this desired COPORIF behaviour throughout the entire organisation.

The closer we get to the subjects we are actually going to monitor, the more difficult the questions get. Divided into two teams, encouraged by Ty to change our way of thinking, we manage to find a way to define suitable competences for all our core values. What competences are we referring to with regards to responsibility? Decisiveness, sustainability, quality orientation and approachability.

The real challenge is to translate these competences into actual and perceivable behaviour. Performance Management, Ty calls it. And since we have already given meaning to the KPIs, we are now going to interpret the KBIs. The Key Behaviour Indicators. What does someone do, when he acts decisively, sustainably, quality-orientated and approachable?

By putting this behaviour on a scale, we can monitor it throughout the organisation. Decisiveness for instance, does not just go from not making a decision up to making a decision. It is much more about the way the decisions are being made. The way of communicating the decisions. Of taking into consideration the consequences of these decisions for other departments, for the entire company and the consideration whether the company interests are more important than the (individual) departmental interests. Besides that, decisiveness can differ per role. To an operator of the assembly lines decisiveness might mean that he will stop the line whenever he signals an error. A project manager on the other hand might express his decisiveness in making timely adjustments regarding time, money and scope. These terms are all so familiar to us, it makes it hard to translate them into actual behaviour. Fortunately, we know more as a group than we do individually and by now we know how to motivate and inspire each other. This enables us to think outside the box, even though this isn't easy. Once again, I am proud of the end result.

Take decisiveness for instance, one of the core value responsibility competences. We have defined the scaling of the visible behaviour of a manager as follows:

- Very undesirable: avoids making decisions.
- Undesirable: lets other people make decisions and makes the easy ones himself.
- Desirable: makes decisions on his own and communicates these.
- Very desirable: makes decisions on his own and has taken into consideration what the consequences will be for other departments.

All in all it does create more insight and a solid basis with which we can define actual and perceivable behaviour, rather than just the umbrella concept concerned.

> *A path is made by walking on it*
> ***Zen wisdom***

We now have a future vision as well as the practical interpretation of the road that will lead us there. We have defined the finish, we know when to score and we have defined the rules which apply in practice. The core values, translated into visible behaviour, provide clarification about what we expect from ourselves, from each other and from our employees. Managers can use this to make adjustments. Manage the performance.

Goal and direction, limits and expectations. We all understand the path and it provides us with the confidence that we will in fact be able to reach our destination. All we have to do now, is put it into practice. This starts by informing the employees and the customers.

> *'The only thing we can do, is give people the appropriate learning experience.'*

'We cannot force people to change their way of thinking, we can only award them when they do something differently,' Ty points out. 'The standard is determined by the environment. As a manager, you determine the standard for the employee. Question is: What experience are we going to give our employees? That experience largely determines the consequence. Ignoring undesirable behaviour often leads to a reduction of this behaviour. But of course, you have to address that negative behaviour in a private conversation. In a group setting you only reward positive behaviour, because everything you give attention to, will grow. People learn by exemplary behaviour of others. A compliment in a group is a positive experience for the individual and has a learning impact on the other group members.' So, let me get this straight: It will primarily benefit your employees when you challenge them to gain the right experiences. Ty nods and adds: 'Then they might understand and will possibly enjoy it as well.'

He continues his presentation and now addresses the attractive perspective for the individual. Not everyone picks up on everything right away. Things like intelligence, creativity, motivation and passion are no guarantee someone will pick up on a change. Managers are a crucial factor because they have an exemplary role and because they need to guide people. Guidance, for example, means listening with empathy, reflecting adequately and participating in a seminar or training either individually or together with an entire department. 'Managers constantly have to consider: which experience do

I have to give people in order for them to head towards our mutual goal?' That makes sense Ty. Which experience do we want to give the RTech employees in order for them to go along with the new organisation? And how are we going to deal with their behaviour, changed or unchanged? Ty is quite firm on that one. He repeats: 'Desirable behaviour should be rewarded within the group. Undesirable behaviour should be ignored within the group and should be discussed one on one. It is not about results, it is all about behaviour. As a manager, you continuously show this. People who are motivated by acknowledgement, are best rewarded with an 'old-fashioned' compliment. This shows them that their efforts are being noticed, which makes them grow. People who are motivated by knowledge are best rewarded by offering them an education or training. There is no guideline for this. It is all about having insight in human nature combined with empathy, creativity and responsibility. It is all about good leadership. And leadership can largely be taught, because human knowledge is about knowledge of humans, and not about knowledge of individuals'.

Experience is the best teacher
Dutch saying

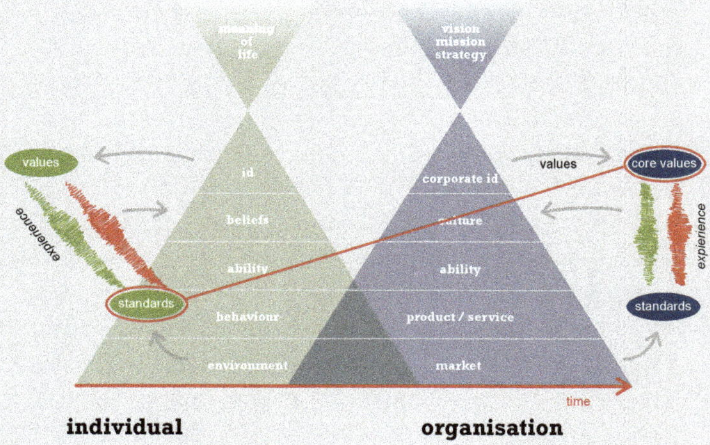

What is happening?

The core values of an organisation are the standard of the individual within that organisation. At RTech the core values are COPORIF. These core values are translated into visible behaviour. The line between the organisation's core values and the individual's standard shows the translation of the core values into visible behaviour.

Following that red line, we cut through a few levels of the model. RTech wants to create a COPORIF culture. This means that the individual employee has to believe that COPORIF is really expected of him/her. The standard is that we expect them to all can behave in a COPORIF way.

The organisation really has to facilitate that COPORIF behaviour and that means that the processes of the organisation, the activities, responsibilities and decisive powers have to be adjusted to their role in the organisation. (Processes of an organisation are at the level of abilities and is also called the ability to control processes).

For the employee, it means that he or she really has to behave COPORIF and therefore it is necessary to translate the core values into a belief, translate that belief into abilities (or competences) and the abilities into visible behaviour (on a scale). That way the employee is aware of the desired behaviour. I do this job, I can take a decision and decisiveness is what they expect. He feels safe in his role and he is able to grow.

A manager represents an employee's working environment. Subsequently, perceiving the employee's behaviour and determining it, means you are setting the standard. Thinking about the experience an employee needs, enables you to influence the employee's belief and this will lead to someone showing more desired behaviour.

Compliments and reprimands are both examples of experiences that are given. A compliment will lead to a positive experience and a repetition of the behaviour that was complimented. Addressing someone on their undesirable behaviour leads to a negative experience and the (attempt) to try and avoid any future reprimand.

If an employee adjusts his belief, he is often capable of deploying all his knowledge and skills (abilities) to adapt to the new belief (and the new organisation). This will eventually become perceivable in his new behaviour.

Reflection

When I work with organisations I always hear managers say that it must be very clear to the employees what is expected from them. But when I talk to the employees, I get an entirely different picture. What is obvious to one person might be really blurry to someone else at the same time.

For the sake of making the expectations clear to everyone, it is a good idea to go through the processes and find the bottlenecks that employees encounter. During these sessions we will build a new culture and build bridges between departments that always saw each other as "the other one, from the other island". Walls will be teared down and we will work together to get better results.

Do you have bottlenecks in your organisation? How are you going to cope with the bottlenecks? Just leave them be? If so, what experience are you giving your employees and your customers?

You cannot escape the responsibility
of tomorrow
By evading it today
Abraham Lincoln

If there is one thing I have learned by now, it would be that a change is only successful when we take responsibility and set the right example. Only by taking responsibility, you will be able to make your own choices and make your own decisions. When you have defined your goal and core values, you have defined the path to the future. Then you will also be able to make your own choices, because now you have a social compass to judge them by. Judge them by your goal and core values. If you take a decision to accomplish your goal and it complies with your core values, it strengthens the decision you made. You might still make mistakes, but that is only human. And you learn more from your mistakes than you would when you hand over the responsibility of making a decision to someone else.

'Do you support this interpretation of the core values by visible behaviour? Do you want to practice these to the best of your capability? And what effect does this have on future behaviour? These are the questions Ty asked me after our day off site. I almost immediately realised that he was asking me to state my commitment, checking my intention and was directly translating this into my own behaviour. Ty's question 'What are you going to do differently tomorrow', has made me think.

The first thing that comes to mind is: Am I still doing things wrong? Compared to last year, I am already doing things totally different. At the same time, I realise he is right. The future is always tomorrow. And it is up to you what it is going to look like. Future sustainability means learning something now and putting it to practice now, so each day you get one step closer to realising your vision.

Leadership is practiced no so much in words as in attitude and in actions
Harold S Geneen

Commitment is of the utmost importance to every MT member, because without it he won't be able to pass it on. If he does not invest that kind of commitment, he is not willing to learn and won't be able to fulfil his exemplary role. How can you expect your employees to commit, when you do not commit yourself? Take sustainability for instance. If sustainable production is not important to the manager, the employees won't actively consider whether production is sustainable or how it might be improved. Ty explains in further detail: 'Without commitment every change is bound to fail. Consciously asking commitment makes room for confidence, makes room for discussion and involvement. Only then they can take responsibility by committing to the result and the team. Only then they can start showing the behaviour that is expected of them. If the behaviour does not arise from belief, the tension remains. Because then the behaviour won't be authentic. Authenticity is crucial to the exemplary role. That is why a change in someone's behaviour arises from an experience that influences his belief.

We all have our own responsibilities. But we do have an exemplary role from top to bottom throughout the organisation. My role as a director calls me to go over the figures during the process. I want this to be monitored. So, I want to learn more about the cultural monitor Ty was talking about. We have already defined all the competences regarding each core value, and we are going to use this tool to monitor them internally. We are all very curious as to how employees experience their own organisation regarding these competences. We ask them about their current experience and we ask them about the desired experience in particular. Should there be any differences between those two, then at least we will know that there is still a lot of progress to be made within the COPORIF-culture, which is crucial to the future sustainability of our company.

'So now everything is falling into place,' Ty says. 'the social compass is our reference towards the organisation's future. Performance management offers managers all the tools to immediately make adjustments towards the desired future. This provides feedback for the employee. The cultural monitor shows the current situation as experienced by the employees and offers tools to develop competences within the organisation. That makes it different from any other employee satisfaction survey. That survey investigates the satisfaction of the employees in their role concerning salary, activities, secondary working conditions and so on. The cultural monitor investigates how the employees experience the core values on a day to day base, whether it meets their standards and what they expect for the future. This subsequently provides valuable feedback for the management.'

After this explanation from Ty, I start talking. 'Start by keeping your goal in mind and start with yourself. Having such an important exemplary role as an MT member, means that any movement within the organisation starts by movement within yourself. It is important to organise feedback. That is why I am offering each manager personal and function-oriented coaching, all expenses paid by the company. To enable everyone to start their exemplary role to the best of their capability as soon as possible. Because this is in the organisation's best interest. Asking for feedback from your employees and colleagues is part of this. Just like receiving feedback from the cultural monitor. It is a way to remain conscious of your environment. When you know what is going on around you and how they think about you, you can act upon it if you are not happy with it. If you do not know what is going on, you do not know what is expected of you.'

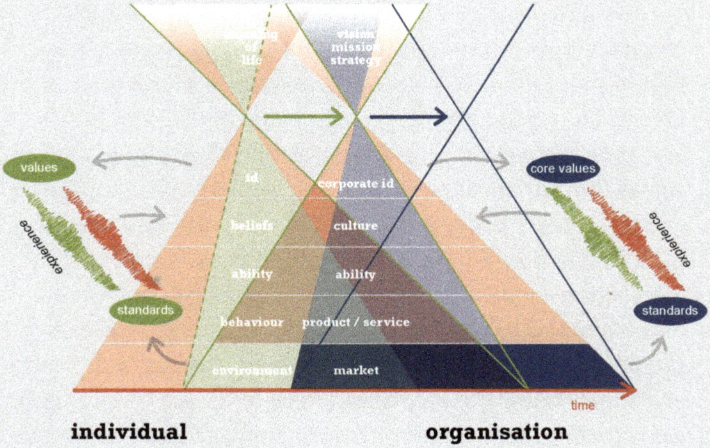

What is happening?

The green and blue parts of the model move to the right as a result of time. The blue (organisation) part moves to keep up with its customers. The green (individual) part moves to keep up with the organisation.

The cultural monitor researches the current behaviour of the employees within the organisation. It also researches the behaviour the employees desire for the future.

If we all have desires for our future, which we are not (sufficiently) acting upon at present, it is wise to make this a topic of discussion. To link this with consciousness, a refined belief and training, so the behaviour will in fact change with regards to the common desire for the future. If you really know what you are going to change tomorrow, you can make an agreement and grow towards the desired direction. The cultural monitor makes organisation development measurable and controllable.

The cultural monitor compares the current situation with the desired future situation. In the model, this is in fact a one on one development. Where are we now? And we still want to keep making a little shift to the right.

Monitoring by using the core values which are translated into visible behaviour on the work floor and by giving the employees the experience with regards to that behaviour, enables the organisation to influence the employee's beliefs. The culture will then have to change towards the desired direction defined by the core values.

So culture can be monitored, if you know which way to go and which experiences you want to give your employees.

When things finally start to move, it is crucial to keep things in motion. At least, if the goal is to become and remain future proof. The right side does not have a fixed goal, because the environment keeps changing. Keeps moving. As an organisation, you keep having the choice to either go along with your environment, or to look for a new environment (market) for the existing products and services. But this new environment will always keep changing as well.

In terms of competences and behaviour, wanting to score an eight is just a temporary goal. Because today's eight will be a five within a few years' time. Keeping the model in mind, this makes perfect sense. The environment keeps shifting to the right. If you stand still, your development will eventually become 'outdated'.

Reflection

What grade would you give your company now? On a scale from 1-10 (1=bad, 10 = good)
What grade would you want to give your company in three years' time? (Please use the same scale)

The difference between these grades is a call to yourself to take responsibility, address bottlenecks and search for solutions together with your co-workers.

You can do the same using the core values of your organisation, which you have formulated earlier in this book. You will eat your elephant one bite at a time.

10 Trust

Employees cannot take responsibility unless they are given responsibility. This means that the MT must actually give them the responsibility. But what does this entail for the managers? And for the employees? What does this entail for the cultural monitor? How can we set this up so employees can influence their own change process?

'Let them do it, 'Ty says. 'Give your employees a say in the analysis. And give them responsibility in the improvement process. Empower your people. Make them co-responsible for the realisation of the organisation's desired culture. This means that time and room must be made available for them to work on this. The cultural monitor is not a solution. It is a tool designed to give insight and to help prioritise the projects that need to be launched. It is my advice not to just go ahead and start with the biggest gaps and deal with all the smallest, less urgent gaps in the end. Start off with some of the smaller gaps; the smaller the gap, the quicker you'll get result. In the end you'll want to define a mixture of both big and small projects based on the results you get from the cultural monitor. This way you will keep moving and regularly achieve a success, even in the short term. That will keep people motivated and enthusiastic to continue working towards their own project successes. Meanwhile, the cultural monitor helps you monitor and refine. This way you'll be giving them sufficient room and responsibility, as long as it is headed in the direction of the goal and within the framework of the social compass.'

What goes for the employees, goes for the MT as well. And vice versa: What is needed for the MT, is also needed for the employees. Besides valuing the competences as defined in the cultural monitor, each employee as well as the MT will translate the core values into visible behaviour within their own role. Thus, adding to the implementation of the change, but especially helping to co-build the creation of the change. To the managers this characterises the change from directive towards facilitative management. Speaking of core values within this context, this is COPORIF-management. This is what complies with RTech's new core values for the managers and their people. This also means that the employees will have to get used to the increasing scope of their own responsibility. The MT remains the client, but the improvement projects to diminish or eliminate gaps will have to be initiated by the employees themselves, so they have visible influence on the organisation's new culture. This too is customer-oriented, result-oriented, innovative, flexible and responsible. This is how you should live by your core values as an MT member and as an employee.

The frameworks have been defined by the core values: COPORIF. The competences are known. What do these frameworks and competences entail for each role? For everyone's behaviour? By enabling employees to come up with this and formulate it for themselves, you not only create the commitment we talked about. It also enables them to influence their own work and judge it. By involving your employees in this manner, you create the willingness to go along with the change. By giving them a say, you enable them to participate in defining this change. You enable them to influence their own future within the company. This lowers the barrier to change and increases commitment and motivation.

> *Act as if what you do makes a difference.*
> *It does.*
> ***William James***

MT meetings are not what they used to be before. When I think back on the way it was, I would almost say 'in the past'. Even though it hasn't been that long ago. I still remember opening the meeting, presiding it and closing it. Actually, I still do all those things, but in a completely different way. It does not feel the same. Of course, I direct and manage the course of the conversations. But the other MT members put many of the items on the agenda. Bill takes the initiative regarding the financial progress and other budgetary issues. Whenever necessary, Ann provides her own customer approach. If needed, Cynthia informs us of the consequences it might have for production. My role as a leader is still very relevant, although I experience it quite differently now. I have let go of being a referee or a show stopper. It is obvious that things are running more smoothly now that the responsibilities have been given to the departments they actually belong to. Understanding, insight, confidence, those are the characteristics of our MT at the moment. A beautiful example of what we radiate towards the rest of the company.

There is positivity as well. We have been working with the cultural monitor for some time now, and responses keep coming in. Responses from the employees as well as the MT members. Especially Peter's department has changed. Of course, I mean Cynthia's department. Her employees feel heard and taken seriously. Besides feeling gratitude for this positive development, I also experience acknowledgement for the adequate way of dealing with this. It is always nice to hear that we have found the right person for a position. That is not only a relief. It is also an insight that needs to be attended to and dealt with. For instance, Cynthia rather quickly noticed that the process between sales and production does not run smoothly. With regards to people and processes, the organisation does not quite comply with the customer's wishes, she points out. She does not just inform me of this problem, she also immediately provides me with an improvement proposal. She has her mind set on a few of her employees who would be able to become sales representatives. During the MT meeting, she asks Ann to train them. Ann's other sales representatives will then be able to focus more on being a customer relations representative. Cynthia is actually proposing a three-way model: customer relations representatives to handle customer relations, consultants to specify the content and monitor the production result and leaving production to the experts in this area. Ann, as well as Bill, is enthusiastic about this and they agree to work out the details together.

Dividing management responsibility and promoting autonomy and confidence has enabled me to do what I am good at again. And that does not just consist of owning, keeping, monitoring and refining the organisation. It also consists of customer contact. Whom I should actually inform about the new mission, vision, strategy and core values. Moreover, what the new RTech can do for them. If coincidence exists, then that is the reason Ann approaches me exactly at that time to ask me if I would like to accompany her to some of her customer meetings. She has received several questions from customers, so she would like to schedule these shortly. 'Customers are picking up on a change,' Ann says, 'all for the best of course. But why do not we inform them about it?' Let us tackle that right now. Besides, it is about time you show your face to our customers again.' I am surprised by her final remark. She is partially right, but I wonder if there is more to it than that. Still the meetings with customers run smoothly. They all respond very enthusiastically. They ask us the justifiable question why we have not told them about the change sooner. Why they weren't able to participate in the change. I cannot argue with that. But still it has been a conscious decision to deal with this internally first and to inform the outside world afterwards.

Rarely have we experienced a potential customer approaching us instead of the other way round. This only occurred when a company needed the exact same product another company had bought from us. No, RTech's existence depended on some regular customers and lots of acquisition. We constantly had to push and pull. It is different for the new RTech now. I did not even notice at first. We have grown so much and taking all these steps consciously means that unconsciously progression is made as well. We receive great reviews on our renewed website, which suits the new RTech far better than the old site. As it turns out, telling people what you want to sell from a product point of view does not really pay off. Now the website reflects our COPORIF way of working. It appeals to customers on a totally different level. Of course, you can find our products on the internet. But the customer's decision-making process is influenced by who we are and how we work. It is not just about technical specifications anymore.

The way we work is far more important now. And it works! We are now frequently approached by potential customers finding us through our website and more importantly, though word of mouth of our customers.

The new RTech appears to be a major success. We decide that all our internal and external communication needs to comply with the new RTech vision, as far as this isn't already the case. So Marketing is stepping up its effort as well, because with regards to branding, they have to be the initiator of all developments within the organisation. After all, they are the ones to give voice and image to all internal and external communication.

> *If you change the way you look at things,*
> *the things you look at change*
> ***Wayne Dyer***

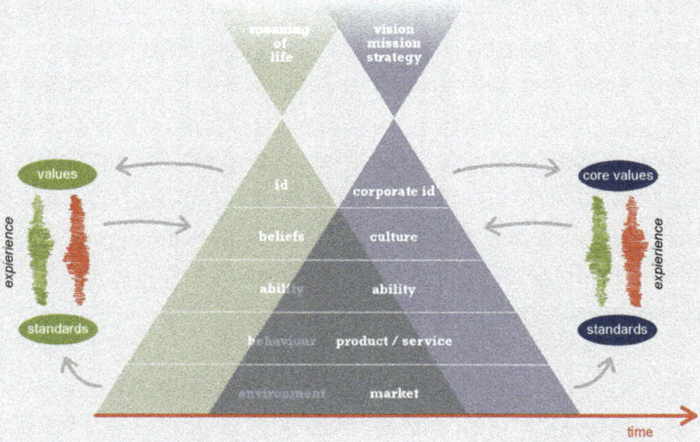

What is happening?

The company is in the middle of a change process to go along with the movement of its environment, the market. This should be dealt with step by step, starting at the beginning. Only after defining your new social compass and implementing this internally using Performance management, you can include the customer in the direction the company is moving. From the change regarding the company vision right up to what it entails for the customer regarding the products and services they buy from you.

You cannot leave out the question how the customer is experiencing all this. Customer satisfaction surveys are a good way to find out. Do not forget to specifically ask them how they experience your company's core values. It is important to check this periodically, before and after the change process. Because RTech wants to become future proof. Customers form a very important part of that future. Therefore, continuing to monitor the experience, the development and the customer's wishes are all definitely part of it.

Reflection

How often do you speak about the core values of your company and how they are experienced by your customers? Would you dare to talk about that in a totally random customer arena? Just listen to what they have to say to you and use it to your own advantage?
Just keep in mind. It is not about you, it is about your company.

I am at the table with Ty for our closing conversation. It is a good bye, but not quite that. 'The intense process of becoming conscious is what I do,' he says. 'I get the ball rolling, to make sure that the real work proceeds more effectively and profitably.' I listen carefully. I am going to miss his insightful pleas. 'We have defined the social compass: RTech's vision, mission and strategy, as well as your core values. We have given the managers the tools they need to develop their employees using performance management. If necessary, we educate the employees, so they can fulfil their roles to the best of their ability. We have organised our feedback using the cultural monitor and personal coaching. And we are well aware of the fact that we have got an exemplary role. We have subsequently communicated this: we have informed our customers about the things the new RTech can do for them. 'That sounds like quite an accomplishment.' And it is. Now there is nothing keeping us from becoming a future proof organisation. My role is changing from actively moving and leading the change to being silently committed and monitoring your results, both financially as well as by means of the cultural monitor. Of course, I am curious what your situation will look like within a few months. But being future proof is a process that should be monitored by the MT, not by a business change consultant.' Ty confidently shakes my hand. I guide him towards the entrance doors of RTech 2.0, feeling grateful for all the things I have learned, received and have been given.

> *Where there is no room for failure,*
> *there is no room for creating new things*

> *Just remember you can do anything you set your mind to*
> *But it takes action, perseverance and facing your fears*
> ***Gillian Anderson***

11 Retrospect

It seems an eternity ago. Weeks, months, a year has gone by since it all went up into smoke and I was forced to start building things up again. Something I thought I had to do all by myself. In the end, I did not do it all by myself, it became a team performance. And it still is. Softly yet firmly RTech has exceeded its old self. Like a phoenix, we have risen from the ashes. It wasn't all pretty though. Firing people, Peter, the intense discussions during our days off site and during our management team meetings. When trying to change people's behaviour, it gets rough sometimes. But all in all, RTech now consists of proud employees. And let's not forget, that is what we see below the line.

I thought I had to monitor results. That people would adjust in the end. Now I understand that monitoring core values which have been translated into behaviour, leads to far better results. Profit increases and more customers who are asking for more and/or better machines, leading to an increase in employees. I was positively surprised to see some of the former colleagues applying for different jobs again. Not all of them of course. That wouldn't be right, because not all of them have the right COPORIF attitude, one that is beneficial to RTech's new culture. Formulating that COPORIF culture really helped us to create a clear vision of our future, helped us to create our RTech game-rules.

The COPORIF-culture has settled in on every level by now. And since we have integrated the core values into the rewarding system, we are continuously monitoring this. It took some getting used to, but the result couldn't be better.

A growing number of employees is coming up with proposals to improve matters. Whether it is about customer wishes, product specifications or improving the working place. People have clearly become more professional at structuring the working processes and keeping them structured.

Subsequently Rtech has become more professional. Customers point that out in our customer satisfaction survey as well. Since our customer network has increased and the customers are satisfied, I am able to say that we have become future proof. Of course, we can always do better, but we have even gained a few customers by word-of-mouth advertising. We have also started negotiating with a customer who had left us three years ago, but we do not have to push him in order to secure our own future. We have gotten rid of the situation in which we were depending on a few very big customers and have sufficient other customers now. Profit is now at the same level as it was three years ago, but because we have more customers, RTech's risk profile has decreased.

We continue to get sufficient technological challenges and we continue to tackle them. Technology is becoming more focused on pro-actively, responding to changes within the technological (im)possibilities. Again, something to be proud of. I think every company that crashes aims for the following: making the change from instability and life-threatening towards future sustainability.

I sometimes just seem to forget that development is a continuing process. Thankfully my people help me keep my focus, so I still have plenty of moments making me aware of this again. Like when Ann announces her resignation.

Ann! She has learned so much, she points out, that now she wants to put this all to use within a new and bigger organisation. It is her dream. I cannot but congratulate her. She has earned it. I completely understand why they want her for the job. This is the next logical step in her career. And now RTech will have to find a new Ann...

We want to tackle this with a positive attitude, so we are going to examine which of Ann's competences we should keep and which additional competences we want someone to bring along in this evolved function. We might even decide to split this role.

Then the phone rings. A business broker calls me to ask if he could meet me sometime. This is a first for me! He informs me that there is another company, unknown to me, that has been keeping an eye on RTech's development. They would like to investigate the possibility of a merger. This is one of the items that is still on my SWOT list we have not been ready for up until now. And now this happens!

I have mixed feelings about this... selling RTech? Just when we have gotten back on track? It must be one hell of a company before I even consider merging, because RTech is future proof now and I do not want to make any decisions that would endanger this position. On the other hand... as an entrepreneur I am not my company and if it is in RTech's best interest, if it would be beneficial for the organisation to engage in cooperation or a merger... then I seriously have to consider that. Patience it is. Let us have that meeting first.

> *The best way to predict the future is to create it*
> ***Peter F. Drucker***

That is another thing I have noticed. The personal growth I have experienced in recent years. From being a fireman to being a fire officer. From working hard to skilful control. From working really hard and pushing the organisation forward to being an example to the rest and making them join in.

Am I successful? Well, I thought I was three years ago. Am I independent? I wanted nothing more than being independent three years ago. I wanted to control everything, because

I thought I needed to control all the others so that I wouldn't become dependent on them. Now I realise that I depend on them just as much as they depend on me. Mutual dependency is what Ty calls it. As long as it is supported with common grown-up behaviour, I am fine with it.

Am I successful? Well... I am happy.

> *I don't measure a man's success*
> *by how high he climbs*
> *but how high he bounces*
> *when he hits bottom*
> ***George S. Patton***

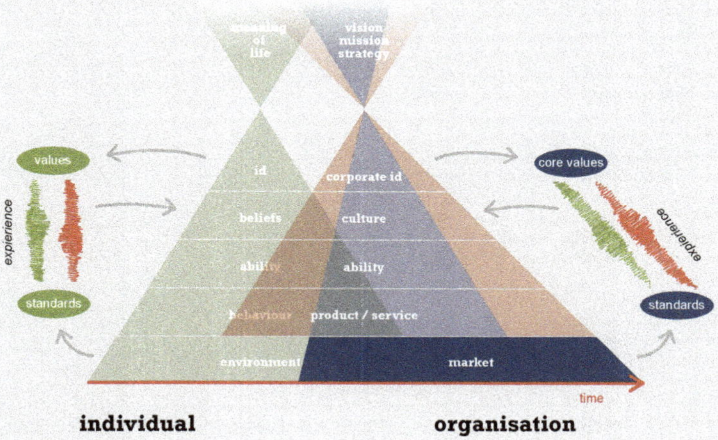

What is happening?

We meet a company named RTech that is quite successful, but has a few important underlying risks. These risks are not recognised in an earlier stage by owner Roy. The first risk is the limited customer base, or the big dependency on a small number of clients. The second important risk is the internal organisation. That did not develop in line with RTech's turnover. It was managed as a small company, while in the meantime 400 employees were depending on it. These risks meet each other and a large customer leaves to the competition.
RTech is not able to meet the standard of that customer, which is shown in the model by the tension between the standard and the core value at the right side of the model.

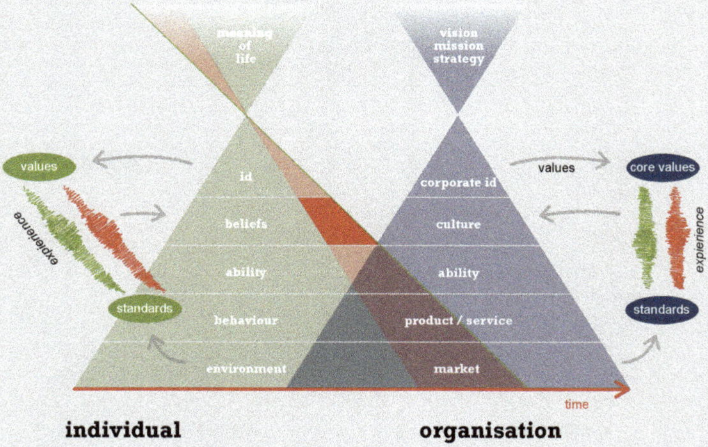

Owner Roy experiences that he is no longer in control and does not have the experience to deal with that situation. He does not know what to do and calls in Max. Max helps Roy to reflect on his management style and personal beliefs. As a result of that he creates more choices for Roy in managerial behaviour. Max also teaches Roy to step away from emotions that block development and decision-making. He teaches him to make decisions based on both ratio and emotions.
Roy did a lot all by himself, decided everything that happened within the organisation, which left little room for the development of his employees' personal qualities. Letting go, delegating, setting course and cooperating instead is smart work instead of hard work.

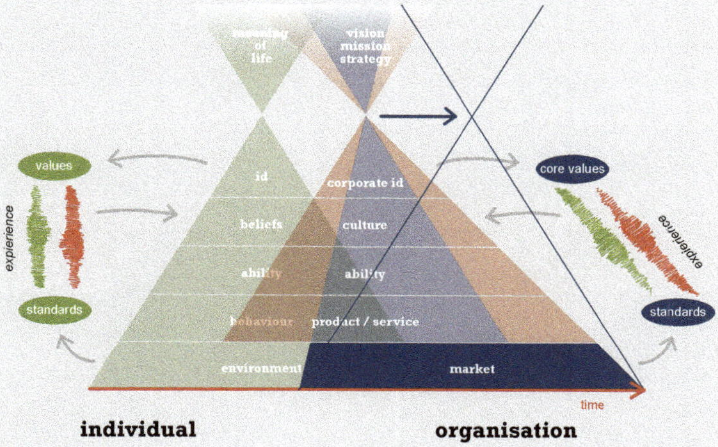

Smart work is only possible when the management team really is capable of fulfilling their role and understands which direction they are headed in. To make that clear in the organisation, it is crucial to have a social compass. The social compass comprises the vision, mission and strategy, together with the core values. Core values are the container concepts that indicate the frameworks of HOW the organization functions.

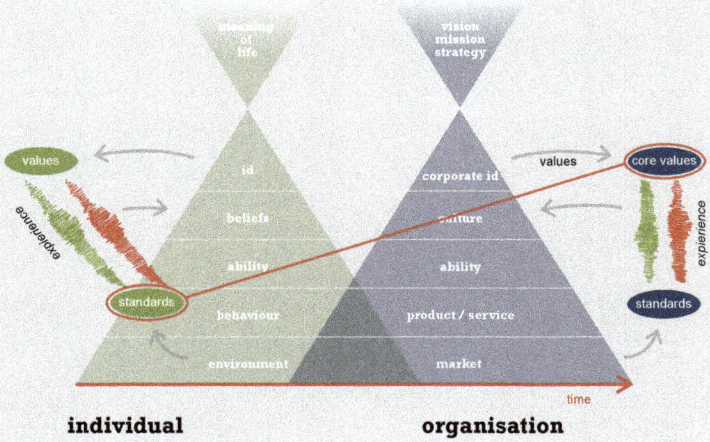

Because of the fact that a social compass alone is not good enough, it needs to be defined. Strategic goals are formulated the SMART way, so the results can be measured and it is easier to modify the organisation when things go differently than expected. The core values are being translated into joint beliefs, competences (abilities) and visual behaviour per role. The SVART way, which means specific, visible, acceptable, realistic and time framed. The moment every employee knows what result is expected and how that result came into being, there is a clear view on the performance of that employee. Only then a manager will be able to give an appropriate learning experience.

That way, the core values are being translated to a standard for every employee within the organisation.

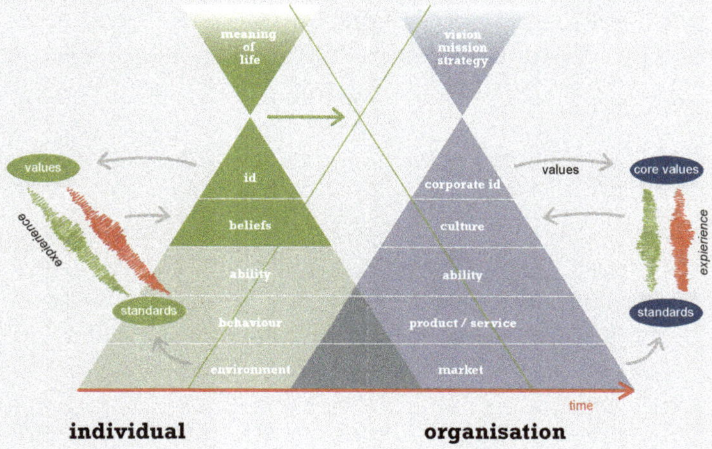

The result for the management team is that most managers can develop into better managers, because Roy gives them room for growth. But there is one manager (Peter) who cannot cope with the new situation and who is not willing to adapt to the new situation. He is fired and replaced by Cynthia, who is a COPORIF cultural fit.

This management team learns how important it is to give appropriate learning experiences to employees. In private conversations, they talk about undesired behaviour, and they give compliments in a group. That requires a manager to be mentally flexible and it will positively improve the organisation's result. Positive changes will happen in the organisation and employees are intrinsically motivated to move in the direction of the social compass.

To monitor the changes within the organisation and their directions, the management team organises their feedback. On one hand, the "what side", they are monitoring the strategic goals using a balanced score card, in which performance indicators are being tracked on four perspectives. Future growth, today's business (customers and internal processes) and past (financial result).

On the other hand, the "how side" management organises feedback on the core values and abilities of the organisationIt uses the cultural monitor, in which employees can indicate how they experience the core values in their current situation and how they would like to experience the core values.

Because the employees, the "who side", are part of RTech's culture, they will be held responsible for projects to change RTech's culture towards the culture that the employees desire within the COPORIF concept. You can compare this with improvement teams that are sometimes active in process optimisation projects.

So RTech is working on three levels; what, how and who. And that gives a balanced approach in cultural change towards the COPORIF culture.

At that moment, it is time to focus on the outside of the company again. Customers have experienced different behaviour in their customer journey. RTech is becoming increasingly professional and that builds trust. RTech's marketing is aligned with the social compass, using website and other marketing tools. Roy is focusing on the market instead of focussing internally. The customers respond positively to that and the turnover increases. RTech is back on the growth track.

RTech's management has experienced that listening to customers is very important and that the second important step is to decide whether this fits RTech's social compass. Only then customers' wishes will be translated into the internal processes. Employees will be more and more conscious of the social compass and will start behaving according to the social compass. If they don't, they should move to another company when the core values conflict with their personal value.

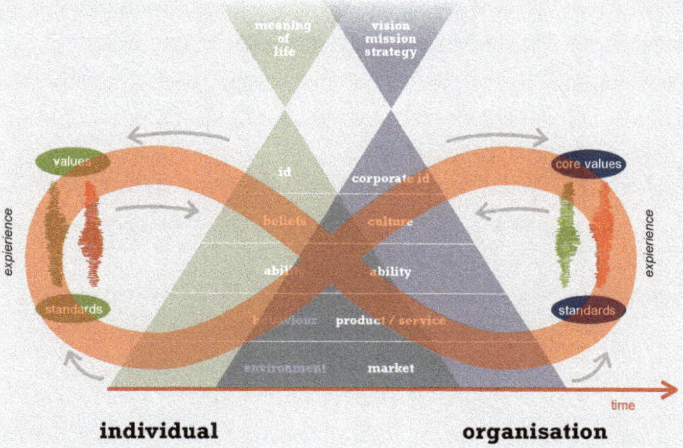

The moment these employees are replaced by employees that fit the COPORIF culture, the COPORIF culture will be established automatically. Customers will experience this and that is why there is a lemniscate of everlasting change in this model.

Because of a big external change there was a necessity to change into a sustainable or future proof organisation with a growing mindset and the capability to move along with their customers.

Reflection

Based on this resume, we would like you to ask yourselves a few questions which will give you the opportunity to analyse the sustainability of your organisation.

You can answer questions by grading them 1 to 5.
1: I do not agree with it at all
2: I do not agree
3: Neutral
4: I agree
5: I strongly agree with it.

Question 1: 80% of my turnover comes from 20% of my clients
Question 2: 30% of my turnover comes from one client
Question 3: Twice a day (10 times a week) I have to decide on things that are a result of something going wrong in my organisation
Question 4: When I get ill tomorrow, the organisation will call me, because I am the only one who knows how things are done.
Question 5: If I am forced to switch activities from employee 1 to employee 2. I feel mistrust and I am afraid things will go wrong.

The next questions you can answer using the following scale:
1: Yes, absolutely
2: Mostly
3: Average
4: Worse than average
5: Absolutely not

Question 6: I can reproduce the social compass of my organisation (vision, mission, strategy and core values) at this moment.
Question 7: I have strategic goals formulated the SMART way, so I can monitor and intervene if necessary
Question 8: I have core values and I have translated those into SVART behavioural goals per role.
Question 9: I regularly think about an appropriate learning experience, tailor made for that employee.
Question 10: I have monitoring instruments on processes and I analyse them regularly.
Question 11: I have monitoring instruments on culture and I analyse them regularly.
Question 12: I talk to customers about their wishes for the future.
Question 13: I consciously say "no" when a customer asks me a question that does not fit my social compass.
Question 14: I know how my customers experience my organisation and whether it meets the social compass.

When you add up all the grades and your score is less than 25 points... You rule!
You are future proof!

When your score is between 25 and 42 points, there are definitely points for improvement.

When your score is between 43 and 60 points, you are in serious risk for the future.

When your score is 60 points or higher, we suggest that you take immediate action.

Gratitude

There are some things one cannot do by himself. Like writing a book, when you are not actually a writer. You do this together. Despite the fact that it is your name on the cover and you have come up with the content, the following people have played an essential role in the process of creating this book.

> *Great things in business are never done*
> *by one person,*
> *they are done by a team of people*
> ***Steve Jobs***

Frank Sensen, who taught me all about the model. Jacqueline Geeroms-Schurkens, with whom I really got to experience the model. Knowing something is far different from actually experiencing it. Harry van Kessel, who taught me all there is to know about the aspects of time. All of them have individually given me the insights I needed to create this model. And then you start to visualise it. Wilbert, you have made an essential contribution during this process! As did Susanne. They now know all about change as well. The animations are a valuable addition to the model. Bram from Foxmountain, thank you!

The text of the book was by Hanneke Speekenbrink, and it was translated into English by Merel Wijlaars. We chose to write it in the form of a business novel. Simply because stories are more likely to be remembered than theories and there are enough management books going around already. This choice led to a few challenges. Because now it wasn't just the model that needed to be reflected correctly in the book, it also had to contain a story that was both professional and logical at the same time. Not to mention the fact that it now also needed a protagonist who would undergo some serious character changes. After all, that is the personal change process. It was a tough job and we have put in many hours, but I am so proud of what we have created. Hanneke, thank you for your patience, (mis) understanding, questions, irritations, logic, openness and perseverance. You have really managed to put my thoughts onto paper in the end!

Cynthia Streep has been a very important counter-reader. She has lead several change projects and came up with some very good insights and remarks. Agnes Cserhati, who just reminded me of the fact that if you want an international model, a book written in the Dutch language is not a logical start. Yet, it is in English!

And of course, my loving wife Terry, who's been my biggest critic. Her approval meant the world to me.

Last but not least I would like to thank my customers, to whom I have tirelessly explained the model and who have been willing to experience it in various exercises. Without their faith in me as well as in the model, I would never have accomplished this. Now you may start reading.

Martijn de Zoete, May 2017

www.ingramcontent.com/pod-product-compliance
Ingram Content Group UK Ltd.
Pitfield, Milton Keynes, MK11 3LW, UK
UKHW061430110926
15112UKWH00025B/214

9 798349 499371